Praise

'*Cold To Sold* outlines a clear process and includes advice that actually gets results. This book will boost your confidence and rewire your sales brain for success!'
— **Alex Burbidge**, CEO, Pro Safety Management

'Before working with Elite Closing Academy, I was terrified to call anyone and ask for a sale. I hadn't asked for a sale in over twenty-five years. The fear of rejection was too overwhelming! Now, with the tools learnt from *Cold To Sold*, I am more confident in my business and I continue to learn and create more sales.'
— **Victoria Dioh**, Founder of Manifestation Kitchen

'Our least experienced member of the sales team added more than 20% to her sales figures from just an introduction to the formula outlined in this book. *Cold To Sold* will unlock the door to the next phase of growth for any business.'
— **Ben Slater**, CEO, Online Bedrooms

'After implementing just one strategy outlined in this book my conversion rate sky-rocketed to 80% within six weeks. If you're in business and want to make more sales, you need to read *Cold to Sold*.'
— **Deenita Pattni**, The Linkedin Queen

'This book provides an actionable system which allows you to grow your sales skills easily – it's personal. Implementing the strategies outlined in *Cold to Sold*, we've added over £10m to our sales!'
— **Craig Parsons**, CEO, B2B Trade Card

'*Cold to Sold* lays out the structured sales process that took my confusing twenty-seven products down to four and provided the first step in working towards my now multi-six-figure business.'
— **Paul Tinker**, MD, The Construction Training Academy

'If you want to continue to detest and resist selling, DO NOT read this book. But... If you want to more naturally sell, grow your business and help more people, drop everything and read this book TODAY! There are loads of books out there claiming to teach you to improve this or that in sales, but this book has the missing ingredient: Real-world, proven strategies and tactics that actually work (with relatable case studies as well!). I love it! I'm a fan of information that is relatable, effective, and helps me grow and solve real problems. This book has all that and more. So please – stop reading my words and open the book. You won't be disappointed!'
— **Jeff Mask**, Founder and CEO, Mask Principles

Cold to Sold

to

Serve, Sell & Scale Your Way To Business Success

MATTHEW ELWELL

WITH NICK JAMES

Re think

First published in Great Britain in 2024
by Rethink Press (www.rethinkpress.com)

© Copyright Matthew Elwell

This book is dedicated to all the team at the Elite Closing Academy, my business partner Nick James, and my whole family.

Contents

Foreword

'Many people see life as a battle; how would it be if they saw it as a game?' This is one of my favourite sayings.

How differently might you play the game of life if, indeed, it was a game? This is why you will love this book and the ethos of the author Matthew Elwell, and contributor and business partner Nick James.

Here's a hard truth, though: it's great to think of life as a game, but to win any game you need to understand the rules.

The game of business, and in particular sales, marketing and business growth, is an interesting and often complicated game for those who play it. Why?

Because they play it with a lot of fear and anxiety, and the truth is that humans don't perform well when they feel the uncertainty that fear and anxiety provoke deep within themselves.

Why, then, I am so confident you will love this book? My reasons are two-fold. Firstly, you will love the simplicity of the marketing game described by Nick James, Co-founder of Elite Closing Academy. Secondly, you'll love the magic of Matthew Elwell's unique, simple, yet super-effective systemised approach to sales. Once practised and honed, any fear or anxiety you may have before moving towards potential clients will melt away as you serve rather than sell, and find a place inside of you where there is no fear to hold you back.

The big prize from learning all this is that you never need to be poor in this lifetime; all you must do is follow the system. I trust you will enjoy reading, learning and integrating the philosophy and insights of this great book and that, in doing so, all battles and fights you may have had with yourself around sales, marketing and business growth will disappear, as if you were playing a game with complete mastery of the rules.

Tony Vee, CEO MasterCoach, relationship coach and author

Introduction

Do you want the rewards you deserve for your hard work? What would help you grow your business, attract more customers and make more sales? How can you improve on the strategies you're using now?

Our vocation, together and separately – and through the Elite Closing Academy, which we co-founded in 2018 – is training entrepreneurs, business owners and teams to get results beyond their wildest dreams. We have identified the key obstacles that stop all kinds of businesses from realising their full potential and attracting and keeping a stream of happy, paying customers, and in this book we will show you how to overcome them.

Our framework and philosophy can be applied to all kinds of businesses, and the list of the industries and business types that are having huge success by following the information in this book continues to grow.

Here are a few:

Retailers, software developers, wholesalers, agencies, education and training organisations, fitness businesses and personal trainers, coaches, mentors, speakers, experts, finance companies, mortgage brokers, health and wellness companies, telecommunications businesses, law firms, diversity and inclusion organisations, dentists, care homes, home and garden businesses, tradespeople, and lots more.

First, Nick James will share the secrets that have helped him start, grow and scale four separate businesses, two of them to multi-seven-figures, and change the lives of thousands of clients.

Nick's professional practice since 2008 has focused on making businesses successful, and on teaching what entrepreneurs who succeed are doing (and not doing) at each level of their business growth, as well as what makes their peers struggle and fail to generate momentum.

Nick has identified eight key principles of business success, the core areas of expertise that need to be grasped by all entrepreneurs, from solo start-ups to those on the brink of breaking through to seven figures and beyond. It's an eight-step strategy for deliberately, consciously and predictably creating opportunities, growing a solid business and scaling it to seven figures and beyond.

In Part 1 of *Cold to Sold*, Nick sets out the eight pillars that support successful businesses, split into four themed chapters covering performance, marketing, pitching and operations. Each principle is applied in turn to help you implement successful strategies at each of the three phases of your business, with guidance on what you should be doing (and, equally important, not doing) at each phase.

Following Nick's bird's-eye view of how to generate maximum opportunities for your business, you will take a deep dive with Matthew Elwell into how to transform those opportunities into sales. For the remaining three parts of *Cold to Sold*, you will learn, step by step, how to close sales – how to think, what to do and what to say at each stage of the process.

Solo entrepreneurs who have to be their own sales team, or small businesses who recruit a sales team without fully understanding the sales role, are not likely to have professional sales skills to fall back on or a sound sales process in place. In many companies, asking a range of employees what the sales process is will result in a range of answers. Yet the same companies will have a clear marketing strategy, a strategy for lead generation and so on.

Shiny marketing and slick operations will not deliver results without a steady flow of customers. To be successful in business you need to be able to serve, sell and close, repeatedly. Teaching people to confidently and reliably close more sales is Matt's vocation, his North Star. He has identified sales as the entrepreneur's Achilles heel, the area where the lack of a clear and sustainable process is most damaging.

Matt's methods set him apart because most of his advice is the opposite of the usual received sales wisdom. Most salespeople start conversations by either pitching or asking prospects about their problems; Matt asks them what's going well to stimulate conversations. Most salespeople struggle to work out the right time to call; Matt believes the right time is always now. Most salespeople worry that their product is too expensive for the customer; Matt says that's not the salesperson's problem: let the customer decide.

Part 2 explores Matt's dynamic sales methods and his philosophy outlined in his first book, *Open With a Close*, but here it is taken further to transform cold leads into sales.

To complement Nick's eight pillars from Part 1, Matt reveals the four cornerstones of successful sales: qualifying cold leads (and, just as important, disqualifying them to keep your sales pipeline clean and efficient), positioning fees, professional sales skills and a sound sales process.

Cold to Sold then delivers the nitty-gritty tactics and mindset adjustments that will make sure you give your prospect the best possible sales experience both before the written proposal (Part 3) and after the written proposal (Part 4).

Most salespeople save their best efforts for the final furlong after making an offer, when they think the sale is in sight. Under Matt's system, there is little to do after the offer (except build on your success), and he will show you how to do all the hard work up front: qualifying and re-qualifying, spoon-feeding helpful information in the right amounts, asking powerful questions, checking and double-checking that you understand the customer's decision-making process and buying culture, addressing fears and countering objections with positive images of the results in store, under-promising and over-delivering every time.

Just as the customer's journey progresses along the pipeline through a series of 'Logical Next Steps', Matt's sales process is intentional and rational, using every customer contact to bring them closer to closing. Along the way, *Cold to Sold* provides all the models, guidance, wake-up calls and handholding you need to nurture your prospect and move it along the pipeline.

Cold to Sold will show you how to create a sales journey for your customers that will yield lasting rewards: long-term relationships rather than one-night stands. You will build valuable happy-ever-after marriages so that your satisfied customers will return to you, recommend you, and ride with you into the sunset.

Combine this with the eight pillars of Nick's business wisdom and the result is formidable.

PART ONE
BUILDING YOUR EXPERT BUSINESS

So many business owners that I meet tend to talk about success, or at least how much they want success, and yet most are unable to provide me with a plan of action for how they are going to achieve it. Some can be heard using phrases like 'financial freedom' or 'I want to do a few hours and spend the rest of my life chilling' – the David Lloyd lifestyle, if you like.

Here's the problem: while doing as little as possible and making loads of money is a beautiful dream, and on rare occasions possible, the reality is totally different. Being successful over a long period and building a profitable business that makes a difference and leads to financial stability requires the following formula:

Discipline + Structure = Success

Don't be fooled into thinking anything different. You can build the life and business you want as long as you know how.

In this part of the book, I'm going to set out my eight core pillars for success so that you can either get started or make some subtle changes to what's already going well in your business.

Enjoy!

1
Performance To Build

At any one time, your business is in one of three phases. Understanding where your business is in its journey and where you should be putting your energy to be most effective at each phase is the key to the philosophy and framework I use with my clients.

Clarity is vital for business growth: clarity about what your business needs now, and what you should be doing at this moment. Clarity on what you should *not* be doing right now, however, is even more beneficial.

These are the three phases your business is moving between:

- Phase 1: Startup (up to 50K). In the early stages of building your business, you're not yet at the point where you're making a full-time income. You may still have another job.

- Phase 2: Growth (50–500K approx). You're making a full-time income, and now you want to grow your business to a point where it's generating excess cash and profit.

- Phase 3: Scale (500k–1 million-plus). You're already probably generating multi-six-figures in annual revenue and you now want to scale to seven figures. If you're already at a million-plus in annual revenue, congratulations, but some of what's relevant in Phase 3 will be relevant for you.

I am going to share with you my eight key principles of business growth, which I call my 'eight pillars'. These are the key areas of your business that need your consistent attention. These eight pillars will mean different things depending on which phase your business is at, so we will study each pillar in turn and see how they relate to each of the three phases.

In this chapter we will cover the first two pillars – Performance and Peer Group – because these are the first areas you need to get right for everything else to work. They need to be the strongest as they will support the rest of your business empire.

Pillar 1: Performance

I was twelve years old when I first started learning about performance. My mum was a trainer for the US coach and motivational speaker Tony Robbins, and I went with her to one of his seminars in Hawaii. I spent my teenage years travelling all over the world to Tony's events. When I eventually started working in his environment, a high level of performance was natural to me.

I was used to being surrounded by ambitious people who were not afraid of being extreme. I knew that I wanted to run my own business and I expected that it would be successful. I never struggled with self-esteem issues in the way that many young people do, carrying these struggles into their adult years.

I count myself lucky because not many people get exposed to those experiences and information when they're that age. At the same time, it's true that people make their own luck, and I still had to make the decision to pursue and invest in the life I wanted.

I still use the mantra I learned from Tony Robbins as a teenager: 'All I need is within me now'.

The Triad model and the zero to ten question

Another legacy from my teenage years spent learning from Tony Robbins is his Triad model of emotional psychology, which I use to this day. Three things contribute to your ability to perform well: your physiology/body language; the actual words you speak (either out loud or in your head); and your internal mindset (what you choose to focus on):

- Physiology: How well rested are you? How well are you exercising? How well nourished is your body? How well hydrated are you? How are you breathing? Investigate all these things to give yourself the best possible chance of performing well.

- Language: What do you hear yourself saying all the time, to others and to yourself? If you keep saying, 'Why do I keep screwing this up?' 'Why am I so useless?' 'Why do I keep making so many mistakes?', that's not going to help you. More empowered things to say would be 'How can I do this better?' and 'How can I stop this unfortunate thing happening again?'

- Mindset: Mindset affects your productivity, efficiency and ability to manage mental and emotional stress, so the right mindset is absolutely key for business owners trying to sustain their performance or build the performance of a team.

On a scale of 1 (complete rubbish, can barely get out of bed) to 10 (on fire), where are you right now in relation to each part of the Triad? I ask myself this question every day, and make sure my team does too: this daily check in never stops, whatever stage your business is at.

When you consistently perform at 8, 9 or 10 out of 10, everything else takes care of itself. If you know you're at a 7 or below, you need to work through the physiological, language and mindset factors that might be keeping you below par.

Are you getting enough (abundance)?

Your mindset is likely to have been set in certain patterns from an early age, and some of these can be hard to shift or even identify. For example, what did you hear when you were growing up about success and wealth?

Matthew Elwell's section of the book, which focuses on closing more sales, goes into more detail about why your mindset about money in particular is so important when you are talking to prospects or clients, but here I will tell you about my personal experience.

My family has always had a sense of abundance when it comes to money. When I was growing up, I never heard Pop (my grandfather) or my mum say, 'Money doesn't grow on trees', or 'Do you think we're made of money?' They were more likely to say, 'plenty more where that came from', or 'money is for spending'.

There are downsides to that mindset, of course, and I inherited a tendency to spend, spend, spend and never create any wealth. My Pop had a great life but he didn't create any lasting wealth either. I wanted to build wealth, and so I had to shift my short-term view of money – my mindset – into something longer-term.

Overall, however, growing up with a sense of abundance and possibility has helped me throughout my life. I've realised that many people don't have this advantage: beliefs are ingrained in childhood that work against a sense of abundance and possibility, and they carry those beliefs into adult life and then wonder why they're not performing well and getting the results they want.

Another common core belief is that 'You have to work hard to make money'. That sounds as if it should be helpful to someone growing a business, but it isn't, because what you actually need is a strategy for building wealth. Without a strategy, you're going to reach a point at which you're working as hard as you possibly can, have maxed out on your earning potential, and can't grow any further.

Making money is not so much a question of working hard as of adding value. Look at the richest people in the world. Are they the ones working the hardest?

Working hard is part of success, certainly in your early days, but it's not all of it. If you want to make more money, you have to add more value.

Whatever phase your business is in, then, you are going to need to unpack the inherited messages in your mindset and replace them with something more helpful.

Performance in Phases 1, 2 and 3

In Phase 1, the only performance that matters is yours, because you haven't yet built a team. If your clients are coming to you for help to improve their performance, you can only do your job when your own performance is consistently high and you know how to keep it high.

In Phase 2, of course, your own performance is still crucial. On top of that, if you have the kind of business many of my clients have, where you work one-on-one with clients or are selling expertise, you will need to get your clients performing at a high level as well if you are to grow your business.

If you can get your clients to work on their mindset and perform at 8, 9 and 10, your business will grow organically because your clients will get stunning results and tell their friends, colleagues and contacts about you. Then you'll start to attract new clients and opportunities automatically.

In Phase 3 your focus should be the performance of your team. Your performance is still crucial as the business owner, as the face of the business in most cases, and as the driving force behind it. As you grow and scale, though, it's important that everyone's levels of performance increase significantly.

I've got twenty-three full-time team members and we are constantly monitoring and measuring their performance. We ask them the zero to ten question every week. In fact, we ask: 'How are you performing right now? What's your energy? How are you showing up? Where was your energy last week? How were you performing? What's creating the gap and what needs to happen to improve things?'

Everyone in the company receives coaching. My leadership team and I work with a coach while the rest of the staff are coached by various members of their teams, depending on which department they're in. They go through all the mindset and development training that we offer our clients.

As you grow and scale, how your team is performing will have a direct impact on the number of clients you attract, the results your clients get, the amount of revenue and profit that you generate, and the amount of impact you're making in the world.

Pillar 2: Your peer group

It's always been obvious to me that the people you spend time with are who you become. Again, I can trace this back to spending my teenage years around people who were already successful but who were continuing to invest time and money in their development.

As a result, I have made a lifelong practice of seeking out and connecting with people I can learn from, and now I'm devoted to connecting business owners with peer groups and mentors to help them become more effective.

It's no surprise, then, that I'm going to urge you to get the right people in your corner as early as you can in your business journey, and to continue to do so. Surround yourself with people who hold you accountable and cheer you on. You need this at every stage of your business, but the emphasis changes as your business grows.

Peer group in Phases 1, 2 and 3

The most important people to seek out in Phase 1 are mentors, people who have already walked your path and who are already playing a bigger game than you are.

My first job was working for a mentor, one of the many contacts I made at Tony Robbins' events. I wanted to learn as much as possible until I could set up on my own, which had always been my intention.

In Phase 2 you will still need mentors, but the most important people to add to your peer group are what I call 'masterminds' – people who hold round-table gatherings and who share values and a commitment to growing their own businesses. It is a model at the core of my business, so I'm highly invested in it. To me, a great mastermind group is full of people who are mentors and maybe also mentees. Everyone can bring to the table some value that supports the other members. You're not just learning from mentors, you're not just mentoring people, you're doing both and getting a balance.

I am a member of two mentoring groups. I joined one of them in 2014 when I was relatively early in my business journey. I was the smallest business in the room and was there to learn and absorb from all the other people. I'm still in that group now and, of course, I've grown my businesses in that time so that I'm no longer the smallest business in the room, and there are people in the group that I can advise and share my experiences with.

In Phase 3, the most important people that you can add to your peer group are mentees. When you have had a certain degree of business success, you have a duty to support and raise up other people, to support the next generation, empower them, and help them take off.

At this point in your business journey, where you're generating from £250K upwards and into seven figures, you're creating more value for other people and making an impact commensurate with that value.

At the same time, you need to keep in touch with your own development. I still have mentors – multiple coaches for many aspects of my life – because I know it's important to have people to support me.

Mentoring others is part of developing yourself because it gives you perspective and helps you see how far you've come. I often meet people who have achieved so much that they've lost sight of how far they've come, and so they're not appreciative of or grateful for what they've created or what they've achieved.

It's easy at this stage to become focused on the future, on being bigger and better, and having more money, more success, more of everything. It's healthier, however, to look back at where you've come from. I constantly do this. I remind myself that, in 2015, I lost everything and had to start at the bottom again and be grateful for every small advance.

Inspiration: From zero back to hero

In 2015, I was running a relatively successful business with a partner. We were turning over about

£2.6 million and had a team of eighteen and lots of clients, but in July of that year we decided to go our separate ways and I had to start again from scratch: no money, no staff, no clients.

I was not in a resourceful mindset: I was struggling personally, mentally and emotionally. I had a wife and two kids, bills to pay and a reputation to uphold. I was coming from a place of desperation rather than inspiration – but I'm grateful for that desperation because it forced me into action.

I had always specialised in promoting and running events, and I managed to get ten business clients to pay me for one-to-one consulting while I rebuilt my events business. I ran my first event in that October for almost 100 people. My vision was to create events that weren't about selling, but more about serving: there was a financial commitment to attend but the event itself offered high value in terms of top speakers and great experiences. This was a departure from events I had worked on before which enticed attendees with free or cheap tickets and relied on getting them to commit more money once at the event.

I had been following the global entrepreneurial giant Gary Vaynerchuk for a long time and he was on my mind when I was restarting my business as I wanted to run events like his. I believe in fate: Gary was doing an event in London. It was sold out, but a friend and former client gave me his spare ticket for free because he was grateful for what I'd helped him achieve in the past. That was definitely a gift from the universe, but it was still a big commitment for me to attend; I was working flat-out, it was a six-hour round trip from my home in Birmingham, and it was raining. I had to remind myself how much I wanted to be in the same room as Gary to make myself head for the station in a downpour.

My friend and I sat in the audience with 500 other people and there was a raffle, the prize for which was an hour of one-to-one coaching with Gary on the phone. It came to me then that I wanted Gary to head-line my next event and this was my chance to pitch to him. A woman four rows behind me won, and my heart sank as my destiny was snatched away. Then there was a second raffle, and I won. This time the prize was an hour of coaching in person.

A couple of months later I met Gary at his office in London. We were talking about his events model and he urged me to commit to my vision of creating high-quality events. 'Nick,' he said, 'how you make your money is far more important than how much money you make.' That hour changed my way of doing business, and my life, because I knew I needed to focus on creating great experiences for my clients.

Gary agreed to headline my next event because it was clear that our values were aligned (consistent values are always important), and that booking kickstarted my new business. We went from zero to seven figures within two-and-a-half years of restarting and I'm incredibly grateful to this day – to Gary, of course, and to the friend who gave me the ticket and didn't get upset with me when I won the raffle. I'm also grateful to myself for committing time to follow my vision when I could have chosen to wallow in negativity.

Looking back, the second half of 2015 was without a doubt the worst period I've ever been through in business, but it was also the greatest gift. The turnaround and the success I've had since would not have been possible without that knockback of effectively losing everything. If you look hard enough, you can see how your worst day could turn out to be your best, and you can see desperation turn into inspiration.

2
Marketing To Build

The last chapter looked at the first two of my eight pillars. Let's now turn our attention to the third and fourth pillars, Profile and Promotion, both of which are connected with marketing.

Pillar 3: Profile

Profile means how you're seen in the marketplace. Can you think of somebody in your industry who has built a bigger business than you? Perhaps they have more clients than you, they're better-known than you, they're making more money than you, but they're not actually as good as you at what they do. Maybe their clients don't get as good results as yours, or maybe you don't think their message is as authentic and aligned as yours. Even if they're more successful, you believe the quality of their service is inferior to yours. Can you think of someone right now? Doesn't that make you mad? It should.

I would put it to you that all that's happened is they've done a better job of building their profile. They're better at getting their personal brand out there, at attracting attention, and so, before we can look at marketing tactics, we have to look at your profile, your personal brand.

There are 101 different ways that you could build your profile. There are so many books, podcasts and webinars on this topic, and so many new platforms where you need a presence, that you can easily become overwhelmed with information and have so many ideas and so many strategies on your to-do list that you end up doing none of them very well, or even at all.

Depending on which phase of growth you're in, you can get rid of that feeling of overwhelm and focus on just a few things that you can do really well.

Profile, Phase 1: Specialise

In Phase 1, the fastest way for you to grow your profile and personal brand is to specialise. If you try to be all things to all people, you'll end up being nothing to no one.

Once you are clear about what you specialise in doing, you will get traction, you will make an impact and you will draw attention. A solution for a specific group will be targeted at their specific issues, so clients of a specialist service are likely to use the service more often and spend more money.

When I started my first business in 2008, I'd been working in sales for a neuro-linguistic programming (NLP) training company and my employer and mentor, Andy Harrington, had trained me in public speaking. I'd always intended to run my own business – it was just a question of when – but I hadn't thought in depth about what kind of business it would be. I had thought I would set up my own NLP training company or be a sales and marketing consultant. When it came time to go it alone, I realised that these were crowded markets and I needed to carve out a niche for myself where I could be heard above all the noise.

I knew that I was excellent at writing email sales letters and marketing materials for NLP or life-coaching businesses, so I offered that very specific service, and because I was already well-connected in that industry, I managed to build a profile quickly. Before long, I was through Phase 1 and into Phase 2.

Don't do profile-building activities at this stage other than mastering your specialism, which will build the expertise that you will soon share with the world. Here's an exercise you can do if it's not so obvious to you where your chief strength is, or you can't decide on the most effective area to specialise in. I call it the 3 Ps:

- **Person.** Target the group of people you want to reach. Keep narrowing it down until it's a number that you know you can reach. If you provide a service for businesses, you will never be able to target all the five million businesses in the UK. How can you market to five million potential clients at once? A business coach is a generalist, but a business coach for lawyers, hairdressers or dentists, is a specialist. One of my clients is a business coach for martial arts schools. There are 10,000 martial arts schools in the UK – easier to market to than five million. If you're a martial arts school owner looking for help from a coach, you're going to want a coach who already knows about the challenges of running a martial arts school.

- **Pain.** Identify the problem that a lot of your target group has. A lot of martial arts coaches need to work in another full-time job, for example, and don't have time to set up their own full-time martial arts school although martial arts is their passion.

- **Promise.** Make a promise to your target group to resolve their problem. My client promises that the martial arts schools he works with will recruit their first 100 members, which puts them within reach of making their school their full-time business, moving them into Phase 2.

It goes without saying that it's important to choose a specialist field that you're passionate about (as well as one where you can see a market) because you're going to have to get immersed in your clients' world and be a cheerleader for them. There's going to be hurdles along the way and you need to believe in the work you do to keep you going through the tough times. You can learn strategies and tactics, but investing in emotion and drive is what will give you the edge.

One of my clients, Gilly Woodhouse, spoke so passionately at one of my events about her work as a business coach for osteopaths that it gave me goosebumps. Gilly started her business because an osteopath extended the life of her teenage son when he was seriously ill and waiting for a heart transplant. She has the kind of commitment to her clients that you can't buy. We'll find out more about her later in this chapter when we look at Pillar 4, Promotion.

Profile, Phase 2: Become an expert

The fastest way to move into Phase 2 is to raise your profile to that of an expert, and to build the perception of your expertise both among your marketplace and among your audience. My clients are naturally selling expertise – many of them are coaches, mentors and personal trainers – but providing any product or service needs specialist knowledge, so don't keep it a secret.

You will increase the perception of your expertise if you create your own framework for success and publish or share that framework externally. You can package it into video training, a book, a seminar, a workshop, a live training session, a webinar. I wouldn't recommend doing any of those things in Phase 1. For Phase 1, identifying and delivering your specialist service is where you need to focus in order to build up the expertise that you will broadcast in Phase 2.

Building your profile as an expert can be challenging because you're essentially selling and marketing yourself, which does not come naturally to everyone. In the early stages of your business, you might not quite know who you are yet, but if you want people to buy into your personal brand, you need to discover what is unique and different about you and how you can be the most extreme version of that.

I am a great believer in the power of the extreme. There are a lot of people in my industry who sound the same because they're all trying to copy people they think of as successful. It takes courage to step away from that and to be yourself, and even to be controversial, but it's important that you do because that is what grabs attention.

Profile, Phase 3: Build authority

To grow your business further, your profile needs to grow to the level of an 'authority'. Again, there are a number of ways to get there. My number one strategy for building my own profile to this level was to run large events. It's what I'm best at; in fact, I am confident that I am world-class. What are you world-class at?

If you're a great writer, for example, your main profile-building strategy might be to write a book. If you've got, dare I say it, a great face for radio, then maybe your best strategy is to start a podcast. My podcast, 'Empire Builders'[1], has helped to accelerate my profile over the past year. Later in this chapter I'll tell you how it also generated commercial value.

The power of the extreme that I talked about in Phase 2 is just as important in Phase 3. You will be more visible, so the stakes will be higher, but being authentically extreme – the ultimate version of yourself – is the way to go.

CASE STUDY: Inspiration and the power of the extreme

Paul Mort, who is famous for using mindset techniques to coach fathers who run businesses, is the most extreme person I know (I mean that as a compliment). Paul creates a constant stream of content, sending

---

1   Have a listen at www.empire-builders.co.uk/podcast52143148

his clients six motivational emails a week, and he's relentless on his socials, but he could do all that activity and still not make an impact if he wasn't so completely himself.

He's controversial in his posts, and he's told me that if he isn't a bit afraid of posting a piece of content, even when he knows it's not strong enough. When he was a guest on my podcast he explained it to me as 'not saying anything in public that he wouldn't say in private'. Most people would put that the other way round, but it means being willing to stand by everything you say in all areas of your life, while not censoring yourself. With Paul, you get the person offline that you get online, so it feels safe and real to buy into him.

Few people have Paul's attitude, personality and charisma, but we can all have a piece of it if we can be 100% ourselves.

Pillar 4: Promotion

We've got your profile established and we've worked out what it is you're known for and how you're perceived in the marketplace, so now it's time to promote what you've got. This is where you need to develop your marketing tactics. How are you going to create opportunities? How are you going to go about getting your ideal clients to move towards you, to put their hand up and say, 'Yes, I'm interested in your product, your service, your coaching programme?'

Promotion, Phase 1: Network

You don't need to be building complex marketing funnels in Phase 1. You don't need to be spending money on advertising. You don't need to be building a huge email list. You don't need to be investing time and money in scalable marketing strategies. Anyone with a Phase 1 business can generate a full-time income from their expertise by leveraging their existing network.

If you go to a large training or networking event, having done your research to choose the right one, there will be at least one person there who needs exactly what you've got. When I started out as a freelance copywriter writing emails and sales letters for NLPs and coaches, I attended events where I knew NLPs and coaches would be in the audience, and I networked and connected.

Promotion, Phase 2: Run campaigns

The problem with the Phase 1 approach is it isn't scalable. In Phase 2, the way to build promotion activity and increase the number of opportunities, leads and inquiries is to launch a consistent programme of campaigns.

To get my business into Phase 2, from £50,000 a year in annual revenue to £300,000 a year, I ran the same campaign four times a year. (I am pretty lazy at times, plus I knew that the campaign worked.)

All great promotional campaigns are made of three steps:

1. Create something different. When I first started out in the events space, the industry norm in the UK was to hold a free event. I therefore created Elite Closing Academy and ran it as a two-day *paid* event, which instantly made it stand out from all the others.

2. Promote one thing at a time and drive everyone to one place: Facebook advertising, Google advertising, email marketing, whatever it is you're doing, drive everyone to one place. The mistake a lot of people make is trying to promote too many things at the same time. The message is confusing, they get overwhelmed, and don't do any of the promotions justice. Do one thing at a time and do it well. If you're in Phase 1 or Phase 2 and you have more than one campaign or promotion running simultaneously, it's too much for you to do on your own; you need to scale it right back.

3. Use all of your available assets to drive people to that one place. Things like:

   - All forms of content and in particular long-form or 'meaty' content

   - Blogs

   - Video content

   - Testimonials

   - Your website

- Ebooks
- Case studies
- Interviews
- Social media
- Books

CASE STUDY: Targeted promotion into the next phase

When I met Gilly in 2017, she already had a specialism offering business mentoring to osteopaths in several different ways – one-to-one coaching, online courses, a membership scheme – but they weren't as rewarding as they could have been in commercial terms because her promotional effort was spread too thin.

We advised her to promote just one service at a time, for a month at a time. She promoted one-to-one coaching for a month and recruited a lot of new clients. Then the next month, all she promoted was her online course. She made a lot of sales. The following month she focused on her membership and made another lot of sales. Instead of trying to sell all the things to all the people, she was promoting one thing at a time. All her activity in the given month, her social media and blog posts, was tied to the promotion.

We took her from 2K a month to 8K a month by doing this. She did other things, such as offering discounts to make a single upfront payment rather than make instalments which improved her cash flow. She's now grown her business to 26K a month, into Phase 2.

Promotion, Phase 3: Expand campaigns

By the time you get to Phase 3, you will have a team to help you execute and implement your campaigns.

We have multiple campaigns running in multiple businesses at any given time. Right now, for example, we're promoting our online events, live events, the podcast, and we've got a promotion on this book. We've got all of these things happening simultaneously. But you absolutely should not be doing all this activity if you're at Phase 1 or Phase 2.

Inspiration: How to add commercial value with promotion

I launched my 'Empire Builders' podcast in June 2020 and subsequently turned it into a source of about 500K in direct revenue. You could adapt this strategy to launch any new product or service.

Launches take a lot of time to prepare and there's a gap between the amount of time you're putting in and the amount of money that you make. A podcast, like writing a book, sometimes does not make commercial sense. A lot of podcasters are good at creating content and technical setup but they don't understand how to get the initial momentum and then build and monetise the product. I was determined that, if I was going to put the time and energy into creating a great podcast and launching it, then I was going to make sure that it added commercial value to the business.

Even if you've already got a podcast and you've launched it before, a relaunch using this model will boost your subscriptions and downloads. Of course, it's also a great way to bring more people into your world and build your personal brand, similar to publishing a book.

I recorded the first six episodes ahead of the launch. I knew that if I tried to record twenty or thirty episodes before then, I'd never get it done, but I wanted enough content for people to get their teeth into instantly. The more downloads on the launch day, the higher up the podcast charts you'll be – if you've only got one episode there's only so many downloads you can have, whereas if you have six there's a chance people will download them all.

For a couple of weeks beforehand, we promoted the first six episodes on all fronts (to our email subscribers, all over our socials, LinkedIn, everywhere), but didn't make them available. Most podcasters record the first few episodes, stick it all up on the various platforms and say, 'Hey, our podcast's out. Go and download it. Go and listen. Go and subscribe.' It's like a soft launch, but they don't get immediate momentum.

Instead, we built a priority list of people who were interested in subscribing and offered bonuses for those who subscribed on launch day – and, to be notified on launch day, you had to be on the priority list. That meant we could build our database.

The first 200 subscribers got a seat at one of our mastermind sessions, the small round-table events discussed in Chapter 1, that our members pay between £7,000 and £25,000 a year to attend, but separate ones especially for them: twenty dates with ten people at each.

Furthermore, everyone who subscribed on launch day got a place at the 'Elite Closing Academy' three-day training, worth £500 at that time. These bonuses were carefully selected to have a logical link to our products and to translate into revenue. If somebody spends a few hours with me in a small group setting, in person or online, that's the best way for me to demonstrate the value of our programmes by giving them a taste. The same with our three-day training. The prizes allowed us to serve our subscribers at a deeper level and demonstrate the value of our programmes and our team, which translated directly into sales.

We also did a giveaway of a MacBook Pro at 8pm on launch day. To enter, you had to listen to all six episodes and then watch a Facebook Live event where I asked a question based on the content. The answer was only embedded in one episode, so you had to listen to all six. The rankings in the podcast charts are not just based on the number of subscribers, but also on the downloads and listens. I wanted to build the habit of people listening to the podcast.

Of course, you can't track exactly who is downloading and subscribing to your podcast. We therefore asked people to take a screenshot of the device they were using to subscribe and set up a special email address to receive the screenshots. It was a bit clunky, but it worked.

You can follow the same system when you're launching a book: incentivise and reward people to buy the book on launch day, making sure the bonuses you offer have a logical link to your product or service. This will bump you up the bestseller list, which is good for your brand.

3
Pitching To Build

The next two pillars are concerned with your broader sales strategy: what you decide to sell at any one time and how you present its value to your customers at the various phases of your business. I won't tell you how to close more sales in this chapter – there's a lot to say about that and I'll leave that to Matt Elwell in later chapters.

Here, we'll investigate pillar 5, Packaging (how you present your expertise, products and/or services in a way that makes it compelling and desirable for people to invest with you), and pillar 6, Pitching. By pitching, I mean your strategy for making sales, for having sales conversations, for getting people to say 'Yes' and invest with you. Again, this will be explored in much greater depth by Matt, but it's important to know what you should be aiming for at each phase in your business.

Pillar 5: Packaging

Packaging, Phase 1

In Phase 1 you should be offering a single product or service. If the product or service is something you deliver yourself to clients in real time, like coaching or mentoring, you will need to have a plan for moving into Phase 2. You either need to tweak your model, or you need more hours in the day.

CASE STUDY: Miles grant, life coach

When I met Miles he was doing one-to-one coaching and charging £100 a month per client. His time was maxed out, he was overworked, and he was earning about £3K a month. We repackaged what he offered as a group programme, which still cost £100 a month per client, but instead of delivering it one-to-one, he was delivering in group format. Then he increased the fees for his one-to-one coaching so that, essentially, he had the same number of clients, but was spending a lot less time doing delivery, and the clients who wanted to see him one-to-one had to pay more. Within eight months he was making £16K a month.

Packaging, Phase 2

In Phase 2, you can start to offer what I call a 'triple package', which means you have an entry-level product or service at a relatively low price, then a mid-price product or service, and finally a high-ticket, premium option or programme. Three options for people to purchase. No more than that.

Earlier this year, I sat down with a client of ours who sells training to corporates. When she started explaining her ten different products and services, I was so confused and overwhelmed that I had to stop her. Her chances of communicating her sales message were zero.

We scaled her back to three options at three price points: packages one, two or three. She had been doing about £50,000 and was on the brink of Phase 2. In the past twelve months she's doubled her business and is about to hit six figures. By stripping back, she is actually making a bigger impact.

Packaging, Phase 3

Only at Phase 3 would you then take what I would call a multiple package approach, where you might have far more than three options for people to purchase.

Pitching

Pitching, Phase 1

Your pitching strategy should be one-to-one. Simple one-to-one conversations on the phone or on Zoom (when you read Matt's chapters, you'll realise there's a great deal to learn about these conversations, but the form is simple). Have one-to-one meetings face-to-face if you can.

Your pitching strategy is probably going to be the same as your delivery strategy. If you're selling a one-to-one coaching, consulting or mentoring package, you're likely to be making your sales in one-to-one conversations. At this stage in your business, your sales will depend on your personal impact, and it's easier to make an impact if it is just you doing all the selling and all the delivery.

You absolutely should not be running a one-to-many strategy in Phase 1. That would be running before you can walk. The chances of you understanding the needs of a potential client in a one-to-one conversation are far greater than being able to appeal to the masses in a group format.

Pitching, Phase 2

As you move into Phase 2, you are likely to have reached a point where you don't have time to have as many one-to-one sales conversations as you would need to build the business, so you will move on to a one-to-many strategy.

When I was in Phase 2, I ran workshops and webinars in which I could have conversations with groups of people at a time. I made videos in which I could tell people about the products. You might have a website where people can find content about your products and services and buy them directly. You're still the person communicating the sales message, but many people can be on the receiving end of it at any given time.

Pitching, Phase 3

Your pitching sales and delivery strategy should now be many-to-many: the sales conversations should not rely on you. My business got stuck for several years in the mid-six-figures because all the pitches were still relying on me, whether I was pitching one-to-one or one-to-many. It made a difference when I adopted a many-to-many approach to sales, when I no longer had to have all the sales conversations myself. I've now got five full-time salespeople in my team who are making 100 calls a day each, so we get to reach thousands of people a week, one-to-one.

A really good example of how the three-phase pitching strategy can work well is my business partner Matt Elwell's story.

In October 2017, Matt set up a small consulting business from the comfort of his kitchen table. He had no clients, no website, no business cards, no funnel, no CRM system, no community, just great sales and pitching skills and a clear vision of becoming a sales consultant.

How do I know this? Because I became his first client. In fact, what he teaches in the second half of this book he did for me. It started with a powerful one-to-one conversation and ended up with me purchasing Matt's consultation services. Initially on a day rate, and then, as the results got better, on a longer contract basis (Phase 1).

As Matt and his consulting business continued to gain credibility and become more sought-after, we formed a partnership together and I granted Matt access to my mastermind programmes, which in turn created more opportunities for Matt to coach my clients and for our business partnership to grow. The way Matt made sales was to talk to groups of experts (my clients) and to offer coaching and training at the end of the talk.

Once the strategy of selling to groups of people at the same time started to work effectively, we decided to build a strategy around making sales from public speaking to audiences made up of my existing contacts and connections. At this stage, Matt was the sole speaker and trainer. This strategy of selling one-to-many brought in just over £500,000 in our first year (Phase 2).

As I write this, we now have four other members of the team who are highly skilled and trained and who can sell the Elite Closing Academy live training and other services. We also have other members of the team who can deliver the training (Phase 3).

In summary, Matt went from being a one-to-one business consultant focusing on selling, to a public speaker trainer who sold annual packages to expert audiences and now has a team of speakers/trainers that can assist him in pitching the full range of services to businesses both live, in person and online. All in the space of six years.

4

Operations To Build

The final two pillars of my system for growing your business are related to operations: who is involved in your business (Personnel) and what are they doing (Planning)?

Planning is our final pillar; performance is the first. It's deliberate and appropriate that these two pillars bookend my system. You need a solid strategic plan just as much as you need your performance consistently at 8, 9 or 10. Yet the stuff in the middle is where most entrepreneurs focus: the marketing, building the personal brand, learning to sell and close (which you'll go on to do in the rest of the book).

Marketing and sales are indeed crucial to getting your business off the ground, which is why so much training focuses on these areas. When you want to break through from low to mid-six figures to multi-high-six figures, seven figures or even multi-seven figures, then you will find that the obstacles are not related to sales and marketing.

I'm no better at sales and marketing today than I was five years ago, but I'm a lot smarter at strategic planning, building a company, getting systems, processes and people in place, and establishing financial systems such as forecasts. All of this is what will allow you to scale up your business.

In these final pages of Part 1, I'm going to share with you how to create a strategic plan. This will give you clarity, certainty and confidence because you'll know exactly what you need to do and when to do it.

Let's start with the people, as you'll need to recruit the right people to free up the time you'll need for planning.

Pillar 7: Personnel

Any business needs people to do three types of tasks: £10 tasks, £100 tasks and £1,000 tasks. All of these tasks are important, but they bring different levels of value to the business.

A £10 task is something that you could pay some-body £10 an hour to do (or another nominal amount, depending on where you are in the world). Basic admin, basic responses to customer service inquiries, data entry and diary management are all £10 tasks. They are not high-impact tasks and they do not generate income, so once you reach the point when you're at maximum capacity in your business, the first hire you should make should be somebody to take care of the £10 tasks.

A £100 task requires a higher level of skill and expertise. It's probably going to cost you more to get somebody to do them, and they are likely to need training before they can operate fully in your business. These include more complex financial tasks, basic marketing tasks such as copywriting, creating brochures, and low-level sales conversations. In my business, most £100 tasks generate revenue.

£1,000 tasks are the things that add the most value to the business. Creating content, forming strategy, building relationships and joint venture partnerships, preparing, planning, leading the vision for the business and overseeing the team are all £1,000 tasks. These are things that you as the business owner are uniquely qualified to do. If you want to be involved in the main operations of the business, you need to do most of these tasks yourself.

In **Phase 1**, your team is just you. You are the marketing department, you are the salesperson, you are doing the books, you are building web pages, stuffing envelopes and delivering your product or service. You may also be doing another job.

You don't need a team at Phase 1, but make sure you are splitting your time equally between £10, £100 and £1,000 tasks, a third each. Be strict about this because they all need attention.

When you're ready to move into Phase 2, the first thing you should do is delegate the £10 tasks and eventually some £100 tasks.

If you want to grow at Phase 3, you should only be doing £1,000 tasks, even if you are good at the £100 tasks and like doing them. Occasionally, you will need to muck in and do sales calls, for example, but other people should be doing almost all the day-to-day tasks of running the business. There will come a point when you can even delegate the £1,000 tasks, which I'm doing now. Then you're in Phase 4, and outside the scope of this book, and then there are many other things you need to think about.

Inspiration: How I built my team

I made my first hire when I was maxed out with client delivery, sales activity, marketing activity and doing too many £10 tasks. I was at low six figures and I wasn't able to grow without spending more time bringing more value.

I recruited a part-time assistant to do fifteen hours a week on low-level admin: managing my diary, responding to customer service emails and inquiries, going to the post office and handling data entry. I paid £10 an hour for fifteen hours, so, for £150 a week (or £600 a month), I bought back fifteen hours of my time which I could reinvest into £100 and £1,000 tasks, which were revenue-generating. Spending £150 generated thousands of pounds more a month.

I added a commission-only salesperson and then an outsourced tech person. Essentially, that got rid of all the £10 and some of the £100 tasks, by which point we were at £250K-£300K a year in sales. Then I could afford to bring in a full-time team and we started hiring salespeople and marketing executives on salaries.

I'm not so good at organisation and detail, so it was an easy decision to hire people who could take care of those things. The challenge for me was that I'm very good at marketing and sales, but to scale the business I had to be humble enough to step aside and let other people look after these areas. Most of us entrepreneurial types are control freaks, but if you want to grow, you have to let go.

Pillar 8: Planning

I discovered the strategic planning process that I use today (in 2014) at a point when my own business was being ruled by chaos and confusion. I had two people working with me – Liz, my PA, and Adam, my salesperson. We had just upgraded from the spare bedroom to the shed.

My natural style is to think in the short term. I can see what needs to happen this week and I can make it happen fast. Not with very fine detail, but I get it done. At that point, though, I had no long-term vision or plan. I'd got the business into Phase 2, but we'd hit a ceiling at £250K–£300K and remained there since 2012, and I knew in my heart that my lack of a strategic plan was to blame.

I was learning as much as I could about business and absorbing theories like a sponge, but the problem was that most weeks I'd walk into the shed and say: 'Guess what, team, I've had this idea. It's going to be amazing. Drop everything. Here's what's going to work. Here's what's going to make the biggest difference. Let's do it.' But Liz and Adam were still getting to grips with my crazy, hare-brained plan of the previous week, which I was sure was also going to make all the difference. There was no certainty for my team. I had to sort it out. I did, so they're still working with me, which, frankly, staggers me.

In September 2014, I went to yet another workshop, this time in Phoenix, Arizona. I'm sure, back in the shed, expectations were not high. This workshop, The Leap Forum, was about how to take your already successful business and scale it to seven or eight figures. I came back and implemented everything I'd learned at the workshop about strategic planning, and this time it really did make all the difference.

From October to December that year we brought in more revenue than we had in the previous twelve months combined. The following year we reached seven figures for the first time. I then started two new businesses that now generate seven figures in annual revenue. Since then, we've built the team to twenty-three people, who all have absolute certainty as to what the vision is, what our key priorities are and what their roles require.

We even increased our overall profit during the pandemic, despite being an events business that couldn't run events. Thanks to the strategic planning process, we found ways to prioritise and keep moving towards our ultimate vision.

I've adapted and tweaked the process I learned at The Leap Forum many times since 2014, and this is how it works for me now. It works for whatever phase your business is in, you just need to adjust the timescales. There are three key parts to it.

1. Vision

The big picture, the long term, the dream. Everyone thinks they have clarity about their vision, but they don't. One of my ambitions is to own a football club. If I bought Aston Villa (I'm a fan), I would need to establish the vision, along with the key leaders in that company. Let's say the vision for Aston Villa FC is to break into the Champions League in the next five years.

2. Strategy

Strategy is your mid-term plan, the next level of detail down, and your key areas of focus for the next three to twelve months. Are there any weaknesses in the squad? Might we need to buy and sell players? Maybe we need to sell more tickets for games to drive more revenue so we can reinvest in more players. The Aston Villa strategy might be adjusted season to season, or we might set it for the next twelve months to two years, working towards the Champions League.

3. Tactics

This is the smallest level of detail. If we're playing Chelsea at Stamford Bridge next weekend, which players are we going to pick in which positions? What systems are we going to deploy in the game? Are we going to go man to man? Are we going to go zone off from corners?

The strategic gap

Our natural tendency is to be good at one extreme or another: either the big picture or the fine detail, the getting stuff done, day in and day out. What's missing for most people is the middle element – strategy. It's rare to be able to do all three. As I said above, you need to recognise which skills you're lacking and make sure the people you hire make up for it. At the beginning, though, you'll have to train yourself to do what might not come naturally, because you'll be doing everything.

If you apply this strategic planning process to your business, the degree to which you'll need to plan depends on your phase of growth. If you're in Phase 1, your vision may only be a year or two ahead. If you're in Phase 2, your vision might be three or four years away, and five to ten years if you're in Phase 3. Even though my business is in Phase 4 now, I'm still naturally a short-term thinker and the biggest chunk of time my brain can comprehend is five years, so we plan our vision five years at a time.

Before you start planning, let's look at vision, strategy and tactics in more detail.

Vision

Vision is comprised of three elements:

1. **Purpose.** Why do you do what you do? Why does your business exist? What purpose does it serve in the world? Our purpose is simply that we develop people. Everything we do within our group of companies is designed to develop people, because that has been a massive part of my life since I was twelve.

2. **Mission.** This is the measurable journey that you're on in whatever is 'the long term' for your business: two years if you're in Phase 1, up to ten years in Phases 2 or 3. Your mission should include three key numbers that you're tracking, so you'll know year on year whether you're on course to fulfil it. For our business, these are: annual revenue, tickets sold to our events, and the number of clients. I've got these numbers mapped out three years ahead and will be working on the next three years over the next six months. There's always a mission that we're working towards. The purpose never changes, but the mission that we're on does.

3. **Values.** These are the standards that you set for yourself and your team. Our vision as a whole (purpose, mission and values) is my go-to filter for decision-making. A lot of opportunities are presented to me, and a lot of people want to partner with me. I always ask myself whether the opportunity or partnership moves me towards our vision or away from it.

Clarity of vision will help you make good decisions when you are overwhelmed with opportunities, ideas, strategies, tactics and things that you want to do, could do, or think you should do. Your vision and your core values are your guiding principles.

Back in 2014, I thought I had clarity of vision, but it was all in my head. It was the best-kept secret in the world. Documenting my vision, sharing it with the team and involving them in the process was a massive step. If you don't have a team to share your vision and core values with, stick them on the wall where you can see them.

If you do have a team and you can get them involved, it then becomes their vision as well. It's my team that suggested using famous buildings, starting with the Rotunda in Birmingham, as a metaphor for our success.

You should be able to share your vision and core values on one piece of paper. You might need a more detailed document as well, but you need a one-page summary to share. Everyone in my team can remember what's on the single page, so they operate day-to-day in ways that are aligned with our core values.

Strategy

Strategy has two elements:

1. **Priorities.** Your priorities should be revisited monthly, quarterly or annually, depending on what phase you're in. If you're in Phase 2, your priorities should be revisited and redesigned once a quarter. This level of planning makes sense in Phase 2, because the level of activities you will be doing and the part-time staff you will be bringing in means that you need to plan further ahead. I suggest setting a maximum of three priorities. Once my brain gets past three things on a list, it gets confused and overwhelmed. I found this out the hard way. In this strategy, we're going from the biggest chunk of information you could imagine – your vision, which isn't even measurable – down to the minute detail. You will therefore think about many things on any given day, but only three should be priorities. If your priorities are not immediately clear, look at the other seven pillars we've discussed and think about what needs to be done in each area, make a list and choose three. In Phase 1, you don't know yet what is going to work long term, so you might focus on one priority at a time for the next month. What product or service are you going to focus on selling? How can you generate as many one-to-one conversations as possible? In Phase 2, a priority might be to build a marketing machine that generates leads month in, month out. If you're in Phase 1, that's probably not a priority. Your priority might be

to create a written proposal or brochure for your single-focus product or service.

2. **Evidence of success.** This is how you measure whether you've achieved your monthly, quarterly or annual priorities. They should be measurable (for example in numerical terms), so at the end of the month or the quarter or the year, you can say whether you achieved that number. Alternatively, the delivery of a project might be evidence of success. Creating and publishing a brochure for your coaching programme has evidence of success built in, for example, because you're either going to have the brochure in your hands at the end of the month or quarter or you're not. Have no more than three pieces of evidence of success for each priority. You should have several SMARTs or projects that can contribute evidence of success for each of your priorities. This is taken from SMART goal setting (Specific, Measurable, Achievable, Realistic and Timely). Let's say you are in Phase 2, for example, and building your marketing machine. Evidence of success might be the number of leads generated this quarter, or a certain amount of revenue generated. Another evidence of success might be testing at least £X on Facebook ads or YouTube ads. Within that, you might have SMARTs called 'YouTube ads', 'Facebook ads', and 'Revenue generation from a funnel' – all the areas you need to work on to hit your evidence of success.

Tactics

Your tactics are the checkpoints, or milestones, throughout the month, quarter or year in which you're delivering the SMARTs.

To look at the example above, if you've got a SMART called 'Facebook ads' because one of your pieces of evidence of success is a certain number of leads generated in the quarter, then your first milestone might be to recruit somebody to run Facebook ads. Or it might be to take a course, or it might be outsourcing to an agency. The next milestone might be to build the sales funnel that the ads are going to feed into. The next might be to test a certain budget by a certain date.

When you've got a well-formed strategic plan, that's where the magic is. All you need to do is make sure that you do what you said you would. Deliver on the milestones by the due dates and you'll automatically hit your evidence of success, succeed in your monthly, quarterly, and annual priorities, and be on track for your mission this year, next year, and the year after. That means you're fulfilling your purpose.

Never stop planning

Planning takes time and attention. We spend, as a company, two-and-a-half days completely out of the business doing our annual planning. We spend a day and a half completely out of the business every quarter doing our planning. We spend half a day a month reviewing our progress towards our plans. This system will only work if you review your plans regularly.

If you have multiple businesses, you need to decide whether you have a strategic plan for each business or one for the group. As my team works across three businesses, the plan that we create each quarter needs to cover all our companies. For that to work, the various companies need to be aligned towards the same vision. When we set priorities, we don't prioritise one business, we prioritise a theme and, within the theme, we include the evidence of success and SMARTs relating to the different businesses. If I had two companies with different teams in different industries, however, I would have two separate plans.

Planning does not mean you have to stop thinking creatively or having ideas. I have new ideas all the time and so do my team, all twenty-three of them, so that's a lot of ideas. We've created a habit of bringing those ideas and suggestions to the strategic planning meetings. The team knows that they will be given a platform once a quarter and that's when they can bring their ideas to the party.

The point of planning is to get a system in place that allows your creativity to flourish more because you are removing uncertainty and anxiety. Here is the five-year vision for our group of companies:

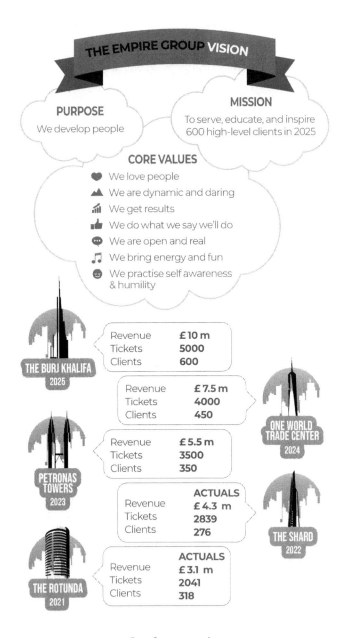

THE EMPIRE GROUP VISION

PURPOSE
We develop people

MISSION
To serve, educate, and inspire 600 high-level clients in 2025

CORE VALUES
- We love people
- We are dynamic and daring
- We get results
- We do what we say we'll do
- We are open and real
- We bring energy and fun
- We practise self awareness & humility

THE BURJ KHALIFA 2025

Revenue	£ 10 m
Tickets	5000
Clients	600

ONE WORLD TRADE CENTER 2024

Revenue	£ 7.5 m
Tickets	4000
Clients	450

PETRONAS TOWERS 2023

Revenue	£ 5.5 m
Tickets	3500
Clients	350

THE SHARD 2022

	ACTUALS
Revenue	£ 4.3 m
Tickets	2839
Clients	276

THE ROTUNDA 2021

	ACTUALS
Revenue	£ 3.1 m
Tickets	2041
Clients	318

Our five-year plan

PART TWO
THE PERFECT SALES PROCESS

The business opportunities you learned how to generate in Part 1 now need to be turned into sales.

Many companies have a tried and tested marketing process, a CRM system, automated emails and repeatable strategies to serve their customers. The same cannot be said for a perfect sales process – a repeatable process that the whole company can get behind. It makes forecasting, scaling, growing and consistency a foregone conclusion. The problem faced by businesses that do not have their sales process sorted is *inconsistent results*. Feast or famine.

Sales opportunities will come into your business as two types of lead: Marketing Qualified Leads (MQL), which are generated online and for which the entire process can be automated, or Sales Qualified Leads (SQLs), which require human-to-human contact. The following chapters are concerned almost entirely with SQLs, although we will cover how to use the SQL strategy to close sales from MQLs.

My first book, *Open With a Close*, showed salespeople how to close sales from SQLs effortlessly using a twelve-step process, known as the cold-to-sold journey. Now, I'm taking you back a step earlier in that process. We're right at the beginning of the journey with a new lead and you're starting from cold: you don't even know yet if your potential prospect is ready to take the cold-to-sold journey with you.

In later chapters, I will introduce you to the four stages your SQLs can pass through on the journey: Cold Prospect, Prospect, Warm Prospect and Hot Qualified Lead. The mid-point of this journey, between Prospect and Warm Prospect, is when you deliver your written proposal. The written proposal is also something that will be discussed in the upcoming chapters. Essentially, however, it is a simple written summary of your products/service, the results it will deliver, the payment options and all the main information needed to stimulate questions, that is given to the buyer just before you make the close. It should be simple, giving a few clear options. If it is too wordy, full of figures, dense with information, and offering too many choices, you will lose them. If you are still explaining things in detail in the written proposal, it's almost impossible for the prospect to come on board.

My system is divided into steps that need to be followed before the written proposal (BWP), see Part 3, and after the written proposal (AWP), see Part 4.

Under some circumstances (for example, if your online marketing is strong and you can get prospects almost to the point of closing online) you can start from Chapter 8 (in Part 3), although you will almost certainly find Part 2 helpful at some point.

In Chapters 6–9, we will look at each category of SQL in detail and you will learn to turn them all into sales, but before you set off on the cold-to-sold journey, you need to understand and put in place some key principles. I call these the four cornerstones of successful sales, and I will introduce them in the next chapter.

5

The Four Cornerstones
Of Successful Sales

E verything I tell you in this chapter needs to be adapted to the norms in your particular industry, or the norm as it applies to your particular clients, but the principles are the same. Here are my four cornerstones, which you need to have in place in order for my system to work:

1. **Qualification:** Deciding whether you and your prospect are a match and whether they want or need to join you on the cold-to-sold journey. For this, you'll need your first powerful question: the Prospecting Positive Question (PPQ) (or for them to have taken a qualification action online, also known as a 'micro commitment').

2. **Positioning fees:** Making sure the 'money mindset' you have inherited doesn't hold you back.

3. **Professional sales skills:** Starting with the mindset of a professional.

4. **The sales process:** A solid and sustainable sales process that everyone in your business understands.

For every industry, qualification is the critical first cornerstone, so we'll start there.

Cornerstone 1: Qualification

If someone has clicked on a link on your website or LinkedIn post, visited your showroom or joined your Facebook group, you have not qualified them yet, they have simply shown a flicker of interest. You still have to determine whether they have the potential to be a good match for you – whether you have something they need and whether this is the right time for them to invest.

Qualification is the process of deciding whether to let someone into your sales pipeline. A pipeline is a partnership between two companies, or two human beings, or two sets of human beings, who, when they collaborate, get results. Never forget, businesses and leads are human beings who need what you offer.

A smooth and clear pipeline, containing only qualified leads, means a great result for the end user, a great result for your business and a great result for the universe. They're the three wins that we're looking for.

You're looking to form a long-lasting relationship with the person you qualify. You are hoping for someone who will come back to you and who will recommend you to others. You want a marriage rather than a one-night stand, so why wouldn't you put everything you've got into getting the right match from the start?

It's possible, especially if your product or service costs under £1,000 (my three-day training course, for example, costs £750), that you can qualify a prospect almost instantly and move them through to closing in minutes. A lot of people are prepared to lose £1,000, but over £1,000 is where they need to build more trust first, and where there need to be more contact points and more nurturing.

How do you qualify prospects? You ask the first of many powerful questions (questions that clarify something for both you and the prospect). Powerful questioning is the most important technical tool you can have on your sales journey.

The PPQ

The Prospecting Positive Question is your secret weapon when it comes to qualification. If someone is on the brink of entering your pipeline, the answer to this PPQ qualifies or disqualifies them. It tells you whether they want or need your service and if they're an ideal match for you and your business.

Once you hit the right PPQ for your business, you're off and running. For example, if one of my team or I attend a networking event, we would say, 'Let me ask you a question. When it comes to sales, and in particular closing even more sales, what's your current strategy?'

If they say they haven't got a strategy, you can say, 'OK, thanks for sharing. What else haven't you got when it comes to closing sales?' Then the process of asking, listening and understanding, while qualifying whether or not they might need your products or services, has begun.

If the prospect were to say things were going well and they didn't need any help, that would represent a really good opportunity to ask for a referral. 'Who *do* you know right now that is looking to massively increase their closing conversion rate?' Imagine if you'd asked that question regularly over the last five years, how many more people would have given you a referral. This is exactly how you fill your pipeline up organically – these are SQLs.

Note that the original question made the assumption that they had a strategy, not the assumption that they did not have a strategy. Making the assumption that a prospect hasn't got a problem allows them to confide in you that, in fact, they do have a problem, and what that problem or need is.

Are you in the right place?

To increase your chances of this process happening quickly and smoothly (which is possible for amounts under £1,000, as I said above), you need to put yourself in the best possible place to ask your PPQ and make sure that your offer is crystal clear: people need to understand what they will get if they invest in you without having to think about it.

What can you do to increase this understanding and start qualifying people before you even speak to them? This starts with the name of the business.

I have a stand at Nick James' events about business growth, with a large sign that reads 'Elite Closing Academy'. Always have an obvious name for your company that makes it clear what your business does for those who invest. Our business name acts as an immediate qualification: we teach people to be good at closing sales. Everything we offer has the word 'close' or 'closing' in it. My Facebook group is called the Elite Closing Group. I'm like a stick of rock (I talk about sticks of rock a lot). You can cut me open anywhere and it will read 'close more sales'.

I call this declaration of what you do the universal 'vision seed', or the number one thing that people would get from you, and the number one thing that people would want from you. The vision seed must be obvious in your branding. You have to give people all the information about your offer they will need without bombarding them with details. You want no room for initial confusion.

To remove the possibility of confusion, use the three Rs. You need to be:

- easy to Recognise

- easy to Resonate with

- easy to Recommend

People need to form a simple vision in their mind and understand immediately how they could work with you, or how someone else could work with you. If someone can't recommend you, can you imagine how confused they must be?

The events at which I position Elite Closing Academy also act as a qualification. The promise to someone attending Nick's events is that they'll learn how to grow their business, which means that the attendees are there because their businesses aren't growing. That's good, because I don't want to be in a room full of people whose businesses have grown so much in the past few years that there's nothing to teach them.

We want customers who have specific needs that we can help solve, wherever possible.

At the beginning of a relationship, the only question in anyone's head is: what's in this for me? You've got five seconds, maximum, to show them what that is, plant the vision seed and form an emotional attachment. I want the person walking towards my stand to think, 'Oh yes, that's obvious. We need to close more sales, so I'm going to walk towards Elite Closing Academy.'

I can then say: 'Thanks for coming over to the Elite Closing Academy stand. First, let me ask you a question.'

Pleasure first, pain later

What's the first question that most salespeople ask you? 'What's your biggest problem?', 'What's holding you back?', 'What's going wrong?', 'What's going to happen if you don't solve this problem?'

I don't do that. I start with a positive, not a negative. I ask: 'When it comes to sales, and in particular closing more sales, what's going well right now?'

Why? Because we're designed, neurologically, to deflect, stall and in some cases even flat-out lie to one another, especially strangers. If I meet someone for the first time and ask, 'When it comes to sales, what's your biggest challenge right now?' they're not going to say, 'I'm glad you asked, we're terrible at sales, so just give me your pitch and I will give you £10,000 now so that you can teach me.' No one is going to say that. It's just not how the 'sales game' works.

I always start by assuming that there isn't a problem. When they've told me what's going well, I'll transition to: 'Thanks for sharing. Now I know what's going well, how, with my help, could you do even better at closing sales?' If they answer that with 'I could do X', they've qualified themselves as needing some help. The cold-to-sold journey can start within minutes.

This is the *Open With a Close* philosophy in a nutshell. Start with the end in mind and work backwards. It's important that you can both visualise them buying the product or service at the outset – then you just need to assist them, through words, phrases or statements, to do it in reality.

Once they have acknowledged that they're missing something and asking me for help, I will use helpful digital material to demonstrate how my product or service will solve their problem. The way I will transition would be to use a recap: 'Thanks for sharing that you need help with closing sales. The good news is, I have a three-day training about closing more sales that will solve exactly that. Rather than talking you through how it all works, let me text you the link now (PING). What questions have you got?'

You can close someone investing under £1,000 pounds within a few minutes if they're in pain, if they ask for help, and if they're at a qualified business event.

Disqualification: Your sword and shield

On the first pre-pipeline steps of the journey through your process, disqualification is as powerful as qualification. You will be fighting your ego here. The ego wants lots of leads in the pipeline, but lots of leads mean nothing if they're not qualified. You've got to overcome your ego and go for quality over quantity. Choose qualification over big numbers.

Salespeople who know their boss is going to ask them how many people they are going to close might give some, usually inflated, figure – say, fifty. They're trying to get the boss off their back. I'd rather my team said, 'Actually, I've got one Hot Qualified Lead and I'm 99.9% sure that I'll close them next', rather than that they have fifty unqualified leads who will cause problems down the line.

Knowing who your journey is for is great, but knowing who the journey's *not* for – the people who don't need or want what you are selling – is even more important. That is especially relevant for coaches, mentors or anyone else who sells expertise. You can't teach someone who doesn't want to learn, or someone who already knows what you are teaching. You want to disqualify those people right away, not after you've brought the prospect on the whole journey.

I use my first book, *Open With a Close*, to build in a process for disqualification outside the pipeline, which is where you want it to happen. When I wrote it, my only game plan was to share helpful information. As I started to grow my business, I realised how useful it was to have something that built awareness while building in qualification. You only click on a book about closing more sales if you want to close more sales.

So I said, 'Look, I've got a book called *Open With a Close*, and when you click a link, it will teach you a twelve-step process, a structure that you can follow every time so that you can close more sales.' Then I spelled out the option of disqualification. I said, 'Please, do not click the link if you have already got a sales process that feels great, that's repeatable, that's natural, and that works every time. Please don't click the link, because you're not going to read it, you don't need the information in it, and it's not going to help you. It would be a waste of my time and a waste of your time.'

I'm telling people who don't need what I'm selling to forget about it, but I don't forget about them, I go on to ask them for a referral: 'Before you go, though, who do you know who would really benefit from this offer?' Because you always want their last encounter with you, the impression that will stay in their mind, to be positive.

It's my pipeline, I'm in control. It's your pipeline, you're in control. I only want the caterpillars that are going to turn into butterflies: happy customers who refer my product or service to other people. I've got to do a great job at the front end of the pipeline, acting like a knight with a sword and a shield, saying: 'Hang on a minute, just before you come into my pipeline, I need to check that this is right for you and that you're a good match for us.'

My company recently invested in a stand at a marketing event. We paid to be there because our product, training to close more sales, was perfect for the attendees. It was full of people and businesses who were good at generating leads online but who struggled to close those leads. Our focus at this event was to give away a book about closing more sales (*Open With a Close*) after determining whether our product was going to help them and whether they would make a qualified lead.

We disqualified many people at that event, and we qualified hundreds. At one point, we even turned away three people that someone else had referred to us because they did not qualify. Those were three productive conversations for us because they saved us a lot of wasted time further down the pipeline. My sword and shield protect me, they protect my staff, and they protect the people who aren't a good match for us.

You can't make everyone want you or need you, so stop trying.

Double-check disqualification

Having said all that, be aware that if somebody says they're not interested when they first meet you, they could just be having a bad day, they may be in a rush, or they may have other priorities at that precise moment.

Listen carefully to the words they use. If you can establish for certain that someone doesn't need what you're offering, then great, they're disqualified and no one wastes any time. However, sometimes people will say, 'Look, I am interested but you've caught me at the wrong time', or, 'I can see why this would interest somebody but not me'. Note, this is a standard universal response at the beginning of many sales relationships. In these cases, just because somebody says they are not interested, it should not immediately disqualify them. Maybe they are just not interested that day, maybe it's a no for now but not forever. You must double-check. It's reasonable for a prospect to take time before making informed decisions.

You have to check in with them: 'You're not interested in closing more sales now, or not interested in closing more sales ever?' Give them another chance. Somebody recently said to me, in a cold situation, having answered my original PPQ positively, 'I'm not interested'.

'I understand you're not interested', I replied. 'You don't know enough information yet. What information would you need about closing more sales now, for free, to be interested?'

'Well, how do you do it?' he asked.

'Look, rather than me taking up your time now and explaining everything, let me send you my book about closing more sales,' I explained.

Interestingly, he went on to buy the book and join my free community where we nurture, share, teach and support businesses that want to close more sales. He then invested in a one-day training that we offer and went on to invest in our three-day training. Eventually, he invested in our full twelve-month academy. You must always double-check. Had I taken his original response, 'I am not interested', literally, then he would never have gone on to get the answers he was looking for about closing more sales and we would never have gone on to do business together. A loss for him, a loss for us and a loss for the universe. Note, professional salespeople always double-check.

The Three As is one of the ways that we teach our clients and students to double-check and overcome stalls, reasons, excuses and objections: Agree, Appease and Accelerate. If somebody says, 'I'm not interested', I might say: 'I appreciate you're not interested, but to double-check before I go, if there was one thing about closing more sales that I could give you now for free that would help you, what would it be?' Or, just like in the example I provided above, I might say, 'Of course you're not interested, I haven't given you any information about closing more sales yet. If there was one thing I could send you that would help you close more sales, what would it be?' Any positive answers to these questions present a great opportunity for you to send them something (a link, a book, a PDF, a download, an audit, a qualification sheet, a free demo) in return for their details, such as their email address and phone number. This starts the journey for the prospect and they are qualified.

More scripts are using the Three As to overcome stalls and objections in Appendix 1.

If somebody genuinely disqualifies themselves and doesn't need what you're offering, by all means, keep them out of your pipeline, but first, remember to ask them that cheeky referral question: 'Who else do you know right now who would love to double their sales?'

Cornerstone 2: Positioning fees

The fee you set for your service or product is an important element of qualification and disqualification. Take an exclusive top-of-the-range car purchase as an example. Most car owners have a feel for the range of financial options available to them before purchasing a luxury car. They know you need a few hundred thousand pounds to get started. Even people who don't drive know this because these luxury brands have positioned themselves and their fees at the top of the market. They do this through the use of images, words, phrases and statements.

Luxury car manufacturers are saying, 'Look, if you're just buying your first car, or you've got a seventeen-year-old who's just passed their test, do not come into one of our showrooms. Don't come in with your £20,000 budget and ask for a test drive. We are a prestigious brand.'

How you position your fee at the beginning of the sales journey, how you disqualify, how you position the brand, and how you position what customers are going to get when they invest, is all part of the cold-to-sold process.

Why your ancient money patterns are not helpful

As Nick James pointed out in Part 1, we all have an inherited or default money mindset. It might well be a negative mindset our parents expressed when we were young. It might give us ingrained beliefs about what is 'good value', or 'affordable' or 'expensive', which are not the same as everybody else's beliefs.

Whatever beliefs about money we have been exposed to, we can choose whether to adopt other people's mindsets. We can decide not to reinforce the money patterns we have inherited from the past, and to create our own money patterns that will help us now. Importantly, remember that your money pattern is not anyone else's.

Never even think in terms of whether people can afford your services. If you use the phrase 'this is for people who can afford it' in your mind, you're projecting your money pattern – your value judgements – onto somebody else.

It's not about the money

When somebody says they can't afford it, that it's more than they thought of spending, ask yourself if they would ever say the opposite. They're not going to say, 'Is that all? Triple it and I'm in'. The things people say about money all the time do not have to be true.

When someone accepts a copy of my book, they know they are going to be followed up by phone and email. They're told that the sales academy investment is thousands, and that I've also got a training workshop which is a few hundred quid. We've positioned the fee. It's important to have these conversations about money options before the prospect gets into the pipeline, where possible.

My rule is that a possible prospect should not be surprised when they hear the money options out loud for the first time (even though they will probably pretend to be). I call this the builders' sigh.

When you say your fees out loud for the first time, even if you've positioned them well, a prospect will often still say something like: 'Blimey, that sounds a lot'. Their dad taught them to do that, and his dad taught him to do it. Surprise (alarm, even) at the size of the fee is the number one negotiating tactic that humans have employed in the 40,000 years that we've been using money or some form of token for exchange, ever since we moved on from 'I'll swap you a sheep for a pig'.

If you have positioned your fees at every stage in your pipeline, the first time a figure is mentioned it will not be a surprise. If you think of your sales pipeline as my old favourite, a stick of rock, wherever you slice off the piece of rock, the fees should be positioned all the way through.

A sale is almost never about money: it's far more about emotion than about logic. Yet unskilled, untrained, unprofessional salespeople always, *always* talk about money first.

How many people do you know who have a house that they couldn't afford, for which they borrowed money from a mortgage company that they didn't know, and paid much more back than they ever wanted to borrow? Lots of people. What was their strongest reason for doing that? Security, owning a home, safety, privacy, status, long-term investment, progress or creating their own environment. They do it for the emotional value of having a home they can imagine living in many years into the future. Most decisions involving money are not about the money.

Let the customer decide

It is not your job to decide whether what you are selling is 'too expensive' or 'too cheap'. When sales-people try to make those decisions for other people, they push the people who do want to buy away. If a salesperson runs their negative little money pattern on me, and my money pattern isn't as negative as theirs, they've only got to use one word, phrase or statement about their service that I don't like or that doesn't apply directly to me, and I might decide it's not for me, even though I am a really good match for their product or service.

Your job is simply to professionally present and position an offer that makes clear how much the investment will cost, what happens for the customer when they invest, the positive experience they will get when working with you, and a clear tangible result that they will achieve at the end of the investment. Your job is to supply enough helpful, logical and emotional information along the journey so that the prospects can decide for themself. Note, when the prospect is making a choice, you are in control and not the other way round.

Start at the top

When it comes to positioning fees, start at the top and then come down. You can easily lower your price, but you can't raise it without making it seem expensive. The first time you talk about money, the numbers have to be as high as possible. Most salespeople are told to start with their lowest fee but don't give them everything, and then upsell them and upsell them. The problem with that is that the end user feels like you are tricking them into to spending more because they can hear the numbers going up.

Instead, position your fees at the absolute maximum that someone could invest with you. You can't make up your maximum, by the way, because if you lie, it doesn't work. I tell people from the beginning that my private client fee is £50,000 for the year (which it currently is) but that they can start their journey for as little as £2.80 to purchase a book. I position my top fee there at the front end because I want their money pattern to be considering £50,000, not £2.80, while I continue to demonstrate mastery, add value, ask questions and understand them better. The way that we teach this is to allow possible buyers to bring their money patterns into the process early. I want to plant the money seed and then carry on.

Great sales is all about asking what the customer needs and wants, not presuming or assuming to know, or using generalisations about old money patterns. The most common mistake I see being made in sales is people deciding what other people are thinking about money based on assumptions and presumptions before they've even asked what the customer is looking for.

Cornerstone 3: Professional sales skills

Mindset matters: The Usain Bolt effect

When Usain Bolt presses his fourth finger and thumb into the track, what is going through his mind? Total focus. He is fully expecting to win. He can visualise the finishing line. He's totally and utterly ready. He's totally and utterly prepared. He is not thinking about the guy next to him who might be faster than him. He uses vision first and focuses on the how second.

He's been training for this big moment for the previous three years, 364 days, twenty-three hours and fifty-nine minutes. To be the Usain Bolt of sales, you need to have committed to understanding the power of professional sales and closing skills, of great questions and great language.

If you go into a sales conversation and you've got no skill, no structure, you haven't practised, you're not in the right frame of mind, you've got a mixed energy, you're not clear on your outcome, then you are what is known as winging it. If you're winging it in sales, you're always going to have a problem. It is critical that before you have a sales conversation, you clear out all hindering and negative thinking and replace it with the polar opposite. Think of all the things that are going to go well. Choose thought patterns and processes that are positive and operate with maximum energy to achieve good results.

Write something down that you're amazing at. It might be cooking. It might be running marathons. Watercolour painting. Playing the ukulele. It doesn't matter. Then ask yourself, how much time do you practise or invest in that art or passionate interest? And how much time and effort are you putting into your sales skills?

Are you ready? The warm-up for a sales call

Usain Bolt warms up before the race, of course, and I have a five-step warm-up for you. You need to do this warm-up to prepare for any one-to-one sales conversation, to get your energy into the right focused state.

Talk to your prospects as you would talk to a friend or a loved one. You don't need a different telephone voice or a special pitch or tone. You don't need to behave unlike yourself when you make a sales call, but you should be your best self.

If you make a call right after doing something else that needs a different kind of energy – you've been running errands all day, for example, and you still need to fit in your sales calls but your energy is mixed because you're a bit behind – then you won't have a successful call.

Follow these five steps, and you will.

Step 1: Data means certainty

You and your team need to know every single piece of critical information about your product or service. You don't know need to know everything in forensic detail, but you need to be certain about the key points which you are likely to be asked about. Uncertainty in the salesperson ('I'm not sure – I will ask and get back to you') creates uncertainty and fear in the buyer.

Here are some of the details that you need to be certain about:

- Prices (including payment plan options, discounts, and additional value).

- Dates (future dates for courses or webinars, for example, and back-up dates if the buyer can't attend).

- Value (other than money, what value can you offer?).

- Terms and conditions.

- Who created the product or service and what was the purpose?

- What problems does the product or service solve? What are its key benefits?

- What is the time commitment if it's a course or similar? If it's a coaching package, how long are the sessions? If it's a service, what are the key steps?

- What is the refund policy?

Write down your answers to these questions, notice where the gaps are and fill them in. This will remove your fear of not having answers and build your confidence in the product and why people should invest now rather than later.

Step 2: Use your marketing rapport words

What has led the prospect to your products and services? They might have attended a webinar, clicked on a link, joined your free online community, bought a book, visited your website and left their details, or searched a keyword in Google that found you. What were the keywords in the email campaign, book title or Facebook advert that led them to you? Ask the prospects who approached you online for feedback on what attracted them. One of the marketing rapport words for Elite Closing Academy is 'growth'. People who want to grow their business need to close more sales. Once you understand which rapport words are already working for you, you can use them to ask powerful questions that will spark the right emotions in the prospect and lead them to act.

Another key point here is that it is often the opposite of the positive keywords in your marketing that the prospect wants or needs. For example, the opposite keywords of 'grow your coaching business' might be something like 'coaching business is going backwards'. It is the decline in business here that is the real pain, and that is the reason they came to your website.

Step 3: Control your thoughts

The everyday chatter in our minds is mostly made up of negative thoughts: 'No one is buying', 'No one has the money', 'We tried that before and it didn't work', or 'Will they be able to afford it?', 'Will I know what to say?', 'Will they be interested?' Making a sales call with any of these thoughts in your head is not going to help you serve the potential client or get a good result. Replace them with helpful thoughts by searching for opposites. Instead of, 'There's no point ringing them now', substitute that thought with, 'Now is a good time to call'. The single thing that has most helped me to succeed at sales is the belief in the power of now.

To help the prospect along your sales pipeline, you need to be in a helpful mindset. Think of all the reasons why your product is perfect for a potential customer, rather than all the reasons why they wouldn't want it. Think about why they are ready to buy now. At the Elite Closing Academy, we teach that professional salespeople will manifest their thoughts, and that is why operating from a place of helpful, positive and high consciousness is critical if you want to serve others.

Step 4: One clear, desired outcome

You should only have one desired outcome for each contact or call. Being clear on the outcome you want (at this stage, to qualify your prospect and get them into your pipeline) means you will get to the point. Rather than waste time on questions like 'How's business?', you'll tailor your questions to your desired outcome. The better you understand the prospect's desired outcome, the true nature of their problem and how you are the solution, the more likely it is that your desired outcome, your reason for picking the phone up, will be in tune with theirs. If the person on the other end senses you haven't a clear reason or purpose, that's when they'll say, 'I'm busy'.

Your outcome needs to be utterly transparent – 'I'm calling because...' Professional salespeople don't use smoke and mirrors.

Step 5: Certainty checklist

Before you call, do you have all the information you need to help the person? Do you know that they need your solution and understand their pain and urgency? Replace negative thoughts with helpful ones, adjust your mindset so that you can make an emotional connection with the prospect and check that you have one clear reason to call them (to invite them to a taster session, to sign them up for your introductory offer, to invite them to a webinar, and so on).

The only way of knowing whether you are winning at sales in the long term is whether it feels natural. Professional salespeople speak and behave naturally, with a sense of ease that transfers to the customer, and this seemingly effortless ease takes a lot of preparation.

Here's the process that you need to use to check in with your personal energy level to ensure you're operating at your best; anything less will create fear in you and uncertainty your potential client. Start at point 1 of the checklist and work your way through:

1. Do I have all of the information I could possibly need at a high enough level so that I can operate from a place of certainty?

2. Am I totally clear on the key rapport words used in the marketing message that led the potential client to this point? Not just the key positive words, but also the pains that they might have for which they need our positive message.

3. Control your thoughts – make sure you are operating with helpful thoughts, not hindering thoughts.

4. Pick one clear, desired outcome – and only ever have one reason for calling.

Once all four boxes are ticked, you are ready to move into the sales conversation. If even one of those ticks is missing, do not continue.

Cornerstone 4: The sales process (the funnel)

Now that you have qualified your prospect and positioned your fees, they are at the start of your sales process, or funnel. You may well have assessed your sales process before, but I'm inviting you to view it as a journey for the customer, and think about how to help them visualise that journey, from qualification along your pipeline, one Logical Next Step at a time.

Your job is to make the journey smooth, with the customer able to see the result they will get at each stage and feel the benefits along the way. They decide how quickly they need to go through the journey. Again, the salesperson's job is not to make decisions for other people.

Let's look at the Elite Closing Academy's sales funnel as an example. It currently has six levels of required investment, with a process that happens at each stage. As soon as a customer downloads the *Open With a Close* book at Level 1, or clicks the link to order one, an automated process starts. At each point, the team follows up, checks that what we offer is a good match for what they need at that time, and makes sure they're clear about the Logical Next Step. The secret to a great sales process is to ensure that there are lots of personal touch points for the possible client at every step of the way. In our business, we have an automated process with thank-you pages when people purchase a book, for example, and human-to-human interaction with phone calls from our sales and customer service teams. This is a better way to create rapport and trust than the old-fashioned sales techniques of the 1970s where salespeople were encouraged to ask questions about their private lives such as 'How are you today?'

Level	Prospect's engagement	Product
Level 1	Aware	*Open With a Close*
Level 2	Analysing	Online training
Level 3	Attentive	Sales accelerator
Level 4	Accomplished	Three-day training
Level 5	Attached	Gold group
Level 6	Advanced	Platinum group

Journey to becoming an elite closer

For the first three levels, we are pouring helpful information and love into the relationship. We want to demonstrate as quickly as possible that we've got great products, we're reliable, and we stand out from the crowd, adding value as we draw qualified people into our pipeline.

By the time prospects get to Level 4 and sign up for the three-day training, we have built their awareness of what we offer and spoon-fed them information to help them analyse whether the product is useful to them. They will have a vision of what they can expect by following the whole training and will already be feeling the benefits of the early stages.

As you grow, it's likely your products and services will require a bigger investment, but I have had people who started at Level 1 – buying my book – and within fourteen days have progressed to Level 6, my platinum group of elite salespeople. Others want more time to consume and reflect on their journey, and that's fine.

It's worth repeating: when a prospect is making their choice, the salesperson is in control, not the other way around. When you're trying to influence the prospect's choice – what they do next and how quickly, that is pushy, persuasive sales, and that's not what I teach.

When you have a clear structure in place and can communicate the results for your prospect at each stage, and you learn to let the prospect make the choice, you won't be constantly trying to get people to do things they don't want to do. Doesn't that sound good?

In the following chapters, we'll look in more detail at how this works and give you the tools you need to offer the prospect choices as they move along your pipeline.

PART THREE
BEFORE THE WRITTEN PROPOSAL: THE COALFACE

The next two chapters, Cold Prospect and Prospect, describe the steps of the sales journey that come before the written proposal (BWP). This is the hardest work you will do in the sales process. You work hard now to have the cleanest sales pipeline in the world and make closing easy. The aim is that, by the time the prospect has received your written proposal, everything is in place to close the sale.

Most salespeople do it the other way around. They avoid the hard work in the early stages and rush through the written proposal, hoping that if they can just get in front of a prospect, they'll be able to turn them into a close. Then all the problems, setbacks and even harder work loom into view, just when they are ready to close.

That's why I teach salespeople to forget everything they think they know about sales and to do it completely the opposite way round. Start by envisioning an end result that both parties would benefit from when they invest with you.

Everlasting love and the Logical Next Step

The analogy I always use for nurturing a prospect along the pipeline is that of a romantic date. You see someone that you quite like, you get to speak to them, then you might ask them out. Before you go in for a kiss, you hold hands. Before you hold hands, you make an effort: you think of something to talk about, ask them about themselves, you make them laugh. Everything happens at the right time, in the right order, and everything is meaningful. By the time of the written proposal, you've earned the right to go in for a kiss, and soon you'll be meeting each other on another date (the Logical Next Step).

Our job as salespeople is to create a nurturing sequence within the sales pipeline that provides a great experience, demonstrates mastery, gives fabulous information and gets people little mini results along the way. At each stage there's a clear Logical Next Step.

Just as if you go on a date with someone you like, you lock down the next date before you go home. Or at least, that's how it was done when I was dating, when there was no email or mobile phones and your parents wouldn't let you use the landline. You couldn't just drift away, promising to text at some vague point in the future. You had to make plans to meet in advance and stick to them, and you had to keep putting in the effort. Always let the prospect know what to expect next.

If the first date goes well, your partner will be looking forward to the second, and even thinking about the third. The sales process should be the same. If you get every step of the way right, you won't have to make an effort to sell, to persuade the client that what you are offering is valuable. They will decide for themselves whether or not it's valuable, whether or not your product or service is helpful. They'll find they definitely want that third date.

At every position in the pipeline, the key skill is to under-promise and over-deliver (how many salespeople have you encountered who do the opposite?). Each step should include a clear promise that you know you can deliver easily, so you can then massively over-deliver on the result.

When someone buys my book *Open With a Close*, which I use to bring people into my pipeline, we have to start delivering right away. We've got to send the book out on time, we've got to make sure that we have the right address and that we give a great customer service all the way through the sales process – this is a critical part of being able to go from cold to sold.

In the next four chapters, we will look in detail at the four types of lead that can enter your pipeline: Cold Prospects, Prospects, Warm Prospects and Hot Qualified Leads. There are nuances, but there are only these four set positions on your pipeline. Imagine the pipeline as a metre rule with regular markings along it. In between these four key positions are other markings showing points on the sales journey at which you will have contact with the person. The unscientific sales world loves to sound scientific, and an unofficial piece of science is that you need between five and twelve of these contact points as the prospect moves along the pipeline. I would aim for five or six contact points, but high-quality ones where you share useful information with them, and where they have a chance to see the results of investing with you.

My process teaches what you need to do more of, and less of, at each contact point to give your prospect more of the results they want. Contact points can be both human and automated (such as clicking on a link to order a copy of a book or information pack). If your business is currently operating at less than £50K in annual sales, your contact points are likely to all be human and it's likely that all the contact will be with you personally.

Each contact should end with you clarifying the prospect's Logical Next Step, which you will then follow up using the techniques I will explain next.

6
Cold Prospect

A Cold Prospect is someone who has just entered your sales pipeline because of an action they have taken.

In this chapter, we will explore what needs to happen to move that Cold Prospect along your sales pipeline to the Prospect stage. Chapter 7 will then take the Prospect to the point at which you make a written proposal, otherwise known as 'the red line'.

There are four steps, or markers, along your prospect's journey from Cold Prospect to Prospect.

Step 1: Qualification or disqualification (again)

'But we've already done that', I hear you say. It's like being double jabbed: once someone has arrived in your pipeline, whether you have already qualified them or not, you have to qualify them again. Double-check that this is a good match – make sure that they want or need what you can provide, and that they've got a problem that you can solve. It's important that they have qualified themselves as being an ideal client, too – they know they've got a problem that you can solve. At this stage, we want our prospects to put their hand up and show humility and vulnerability, to shed any denial that they might have been holding on to. I demonstrated in the previous chapter that we can disqualify people who don't need what we can offer, and that it's a positive step to disqualify such people.

Revisit the section on Qualification in Chapter 5 and ask yourself those questions again. How are you qualifying your prospects and what are you learning about them in the process? Revisit what happened before you got the prospect into your pipeline. What was the Logical Next Step they took to get here? Bought a book, joined a Facebook group, or clicked on a link on your website? What more do you know about them? Revisit your marketing rapport words. Can you add any to the list?

Step 2: The MAN
(Money, Authority, Need)

Once the prospect is in your pipeline and you have qualified or requalified them, you need to check that you have found your MAN. This is the decision-maker who has everything you need to close the sale: the Money, Authority and Need for your product or service. Finding and talking to the MAN is your biggest task in this section of the pipeline.

After I have qualified prospects and given or sent them a copy of my book about closing more sales, my team who make the follow-up calls are trained to check that they are taking the right person on the sales journey; the person who can make the decision to buy.

Identifying the MAN is the only step I insist on repeating four times, at each stage in the pipeline, as it can wreck your hard work at the last minute if you don't deal with the decision-maker from the beginning. Check at every stage that they are still the decision-maker, and check that you know the customer's decision-making process. Don't leave it till the close to find out that you have not been dealing with the decision-maker after all, when the prospect says, 'Oh, it all sounds great, but I need to speak to my partner'.

If you're dealing with middlemen and women, you are going to have a very painful sales career. Middlemen and women have learned to send the following email: 'I've shown it to the MD and they liked it. However, we've decided to go down another route and we'll keep you on file.' That's code for, 'I did not present your product or service to the CEO. The CEO has barely looked at it, if at all, and we don't see your product or service as a solution for us.'

The more conversations you have with people who are not directly responsible for the final decision, or at least who are not a significant part of the decision-making process, the more time you'll waste, and the more emails like this you will have to read.

Everyone in business has had experiences like this, but if you always make sure you're talking to the decision-maker, you will stop having them. If you're a sole entrepreneur dealing with a small to medium-sized business, and the amount involved is less than £1,000, you can probably deal with the MAN from the beginning. It's likely that the decision-maker will be one person (though not always the most obvious person, so you still need to check).

If more than £1,000 is involved, there is likely to be more than one decision-maker. For larger companies and corporations the process is more complex (we will explore it in more depth in the next chapter) but you do need to start trying to understand it from the beginning to save yourself from being constantly knocked back because you don't know how the system works. The process for a commercial property deal I once made with a supermarket chain took me seven years, to give you an idea.

Once you have found your MAN, you need to have a conversation. The best way to do this is to connect with them on LinkedIn, send them a letter or whatever it may be to start the process of connecting with them. This may involve cold calling them, and some tips for making these calls and scripts you can use are provided in the appendices. Remember: always give them the ability to move back towards you by taking an action (such as clicking on a link, requesting a helpful online tool or asking for a call with you) – and give them the option to unsubscribe.

Step 3: The free catch

The free catch is something that you can offer your qualified but Cold Prospect, who you have established is your MAN, in return for an agreed next step. Other people call it a hook, to catch a fish in your net. You might offer a free webinar training session, for example, but they've got to download or click something to show interest, or they have to give you an email address or a phone number.

Step 4: The Logical Next Step (or not)

Never finish a sales conversation without telling the prospect what will happen next. Lock down a time for when you will next speak and leave them expecting a call. When my team follow up with someone who has been given or ordered a copy of my book, they will invite them to a free training session about closing more sales.

If it becomes clear to you that you and the Cold Prospect are not a good match, your Logical Next Step is to get out your sword and shield and get them out of your pipeline, not forgetting to ask for a referral, of course: 'Before I go, who do you know who would love to double their sales?'

7
Prospect

Just imagine

At this stage, your Cold Prospect is a caterpillar. It's painful for a caterpillar to become a beautiful butterfly. The caterpillar must eat itself from the inside out on its journey. If it doesn't, it'll never become a butterfly.

Your Cold Prospect is also working hard on their journey along your pipeline, arming themselves with all the tools and information they need. Before you make a written proposal, it's critical that you have given them absolutely everything they could possibly need to make an informed decision. This is where you continue earning the right to send the prospect your written proposal, doing all your hard work before that red line.

You must plant the vision, then start at the end and work backwards. 'Just Imagine' is a technique I often use to help prospects fast forward to see the benefits they will enjoy if they invest with you.

Try it on yourself. Imagine yourself as a new customer and that you've just signed a contract with yourself (as in, the actual you), and you've got the product, service or experience you wanted, or whatever it was that drew you towards yourself. Imagine you were getting the results now.

Then take a step backwards in your journey and imagine that you're just at the point of considering investing in yourself. What would you need to help you move forward? What would you have to do to get the results you want? What would you want to know? That's the stage your Cold Prospect is at now.

By the end of this chapter, you will have a sense of how to tell whether your prospect, by the time they get your written proposal, is ready to go ahead with you. My experience says you cannot be 100% certain (when I asked my wife Kerry to marry me, I was only 99% sure that she would say yes, but I'd done the hard work to be that certain).

Back to the MAN and enter the SQUID

Before you move on, once again double-check that you are dealing with the decision-maker and ask questions so that you can understand their process for deciding. If the investment is more than £1,000, or there is more than one decision-maker, you'll find more detailed guidance at the end of this chapter.

The system I use in this part of the sales journey is called SQUID: Share, Question, Understand, Inform, Decide.

SQUID ensures that, before you present a written proposal, you have covered all the bases to make success 99% certain. If there is anything from this stage in the sales journey that doesn't quite stack up, however small, I promise you it will rear its ugly head when you come to the close.

We'll look at each stage of SQUID in turn. When you are taking a prospect through this process, make notes at every stage. Write down what the prospect says so that you can repeat words, phrases and whole sentences. These are your rapport words, and you never stop gathering more.

Share

Sharing means making the prospect aware. Make them aware of the results that your product, service or experience can bring, planting a vision of how you will provide what they need. Include the positioning of fees, which you will have introduced at the qualifying stage.

This also means making them aware of what's going to happen next on the journey. As I have mentioned, when someone accepts a copy of my book, we tell them that they're on the journey and they'll get a follow-up call and emails from us, and that the results they want will come at the end of the journey when they have completed my training.

Sharing doesn't mean explaining all the features and benefits of the thing you're selling. At this stage, the urge is to explain everything in detail, to talk a lot about your product or service, but if you start explaining what you think the prospect needs before they've told you, you are working from an assumption or a presumption. You are telling strangers things about themselves that you can't possibly know, and a salesperson who does that makes customers run for the hills.

Instead, you should be asking the prospect what they need, and what would make the biggest difference to them. Which brings me to the next stage.

Question

Ask a lot of questions, but only one at a time. I have a ten-second rule: for every ten seconds of explaining, you have to ask a question. You can ask the same question repeatedly if it continues to bring you new information each time and brings the prospect closer to seeing why they should invest. Let me show you how I talk to a prospect.

Prospect: So, what happens on the coaching days?

Me: Fabulous question. We'll teach you the Elite Closing Academy formula. Make it bespoke to you so you can close more sales. What else do you need to know?

Prospect: How many other businesses are in the room?

Me: There's eighty of us. What else do you need to know?

Prospect: How much time do I get with you?

Me: The package over twelve months is specifically designed to give you access to all areas, 24-7-365. What other questions do you have?

Prospect: What kind of results do you get for your clients?

Me: Great question. On average, we increase sales by 64%. What else do you need to know?

Note that I'm not explaining, I'm answering questions. Every time I give a piece of information, I ask a question – always the same one: what else do they need from me? Listen carefully to each answer and keep replying with useful information and another powerful question. 'What else?' is a powerful question; it assumes the prospect has more to tell you.

Here's how not to do it:

> **Prospect:** So, what happens on the coaching days?
> **Me:** Yeah, so, what happens is, for people, like, businesses like yours, what we do is, well, firstly, I do quite a few things about confidence and mindset. Then, once your mindset and your confidence are up, because obviously, in a business like yours, you need confidence, we...
> **Prospect:** I'm bored.

If you find yourself giving long explanations in long sentences, you're losing. Of course, you need to do some explaining. In the first example I explained what happens on my coaching days, but I shared specific information one piece at a time in response to the prospect's questions. My job is to give them the information they have asked for, no more and no less, containing the vision seed of the end result (closing more sales).

Understand

Commit to understanding your prospect when you're selling to them. Never judge somebody's answer to your question. You are not there to judge whether another human being is right or wrong, and you're not there to embarrass or insult them.

Perhaps somebody gives you a green-light answer that qualifies them ('I want to lose weight', 'I want to get fit', 'I want to close more sales'). Do not – please do not – stick the knife in at this point. If someone says, 'Oh yeah, I'm not very good at closing', I don't say, 'Right, well that's why you need me, and if you don't hire me your business is going to go down'. You'll be tempted to say something like that, but don't. Never judge, just gather more information: 'What in particular concerns you?'

The other rule at the Understanding stage is to never stop at the prospect's first answer. If they have said they need to lose weight, and you ask them for their number one issue, they might say, 'I eat pretty well, but...' They're not going to say they're addicted to sugar and stuff themselves with chocolate when the family is in bed. They're not going to confide in you to that extent yet, because you're still a stranger. You don't accept their first answer, but you don't tell them you're not accepting it. You don't say, 'Look, you obviously can't be eating well because you're overweight. Look at the size of you.' (You wouldn't say that, would you?)

The prospect's first reply is likely to be a lie or a defence mechanism. You're a salesperson; they are programmed to defend themselves against you. As we discussed back in Chapter 5, under Qualification, no one is going to say: 'I'm terrible at X. Let me just give you a ton of money.' Always expect to be given a deferred truth. Keep asking, 'What else?' Unpack what they're saying. Gather more information: 'Given that you eat pretty well, which foods currently present particular issues for you?'

Don't get into conflict with the prospect over that first reply. You can't close when you're in conflict. Don't open the prospect's wounds; that's not the salesperson's job. We'll go on to cover PUNT with a Q, which is when you help the prospect to open their own wounds.

Inform

Inform yourself. Gather information at every stage by sharing, listening and understanding, so you never use assumption or presumption. If you say one thing from a place of assumption or a presumption that the prospect doesn't like, it's all over.

From a client's perspective, our job is to share enough helpful information all the way through the process to support, assist and enable the buyer to make an informed decision. We are looking to avoid creating buyer's remorse by creating non-buyers remorse.

Decide

The first big decision you made was whether to qualify your prospect and let them into your pipeline. Your next big decision comes now, before sending them a written proposal. You need to decide, from the information you've gathered about each other, whether you both believe that you're a good match. Can you get them the results they need? Yes or no?

If it's a no, it's time to either find out more information with a qualitative question (what is the one thing you could do for them that could turn their no into a yes?) or to take them out of your pipeline and become a stakeholder for somebody else's business. If you're satisfied it's a no and that they don't need what you do, then send them to somebody you know who can help them get what they need.

The last thing you do in the sales relationship is what the prospect will remember. If they say no and you spend half an hour trying to convince them they're wrong and trying to persuade them to say yes, they will have a bad memory of you. If, however, the last thing you do is help them get what they need, even if not from you (the flip side of the cheeky referral question in Chapter 5), you will leave them with a positive feeling, which can only benefit you in the future.

More often than not you'll be unsure whether it's yes or no, so before you can decide you'll need to ask more powerful questions to gather all the data that you need. Let's move on to the number one prospecting system that I teach.

PUNT with a Q

This section shows you how to ask the questions that will help the prospect find the truth for themselves, removing the need for you to sell. Your questions should establish the prospect's Pain (the problem that they need you to solve) or Pleasure (the results they want from investing with you), their level of Urgency, and the specifics of what they Need to happen next (and what they Need from you), while all the time building Trust between you.

The Q stands for Qualitative – questions that invite answers that you can measure and that will help you gather useful data. Keep asking qualitative questions until you have all the data you need. The Q is the most powerful part of my system because it really gets to the truth of the matter. Here are some suggestions of powerful qualitative questions in each category that will get helpful specific answers.

Pain/Pleasure

- What results would you need to get in the first twelve weeks for this to be the greatest investment you've ever made?

- What performance indicators would we need to put in place to ensure we are achieving improved results?

- What financial implications are there now as a result of not having [XYZ]?

- What have you seen or heard about us which, when executed in your business, would solve challenges or get even better results?

Urgency

- What is going to happen if you don't solve this?

- How critical is this to resolve right now?

- How many more [XYZ] would you need to solve this?

- How many months have you been experiencing this?

- How many more months can you afford to have this problem?

If you're selling something nonessential but pleasurable, like a holiday, you can still focus on urgency:

- How long have you wanted to travel to Jamaica?

- When was the last time you had a holiday?

- How does it feel not having taken the trip you want to take?

Need

- What do you think you need from us right now?

- If you could put your finger on the one thing you need to change, what would it be?

- Other than money, what one thing must change, in your view?

- If we could gift you a piece of information now that would help, what would it be?

Trust

- Other than money, think of five other reasons why this would be a good deal.

- Who else would benefit?

- What do you know about our results with other people?

- Which one of our previous partners would you like me to put you in touch with before we do business together?

- Aside from money, what question can you ask about our company's values that is important for you to understand before choosing us?

Trust doesn't exist in the future, because the future isn't real. Deciding to trust someone is a decision that needs to be made in the moment, now, because you have to trust someone now and they have to trust you. This system teaches you to trust and be trustworthy.

I used to deal with builders and when we talked about money it would sound something like this:

> **Builder:** 'The quote is £16,000. I take £6,000 on account. I take the rest in thirty days.'
> **Me:** 'Don't you trust me?'
> **Builder:** 'Of course I trust you. Now it's your turn to trust me with your six grand.'

If a prospect asks if you trust them, always agree. 'Of course I trust you. Now it's your turn to trust me.'

When you are asking these powerful questions, prepare to encounter all the prospect's defences, especially if you're looking for an investment of more than £1,000. You're going to get stalls and reasons why they shouldn't invest. You have to stay strong. Because I'm going to give you your next secret weapon. It's called RIO (Minus and Plus).

A trip to RIO: What prospects need to hear

People generally see problems first. If your prospect is in a state of fear, they will only be able to see problems. You have to unpack the prospect's fear, examine it and deal with it. It's worth it: amazing things happen on the other side of fear. Also, if you don't see off the fear properly, it will come back to haunt you at the close. When you hear comments like, 'I need to ask my partner' or 'pop it in an email', it's a sign that fear is still lurking and that you haven't dealt with it fully.

RIO is my system for banishing fear. I created RIO Minus and RIO Plus (to be used in that order) because most salespeople are not prepared to listen to the prospect being scared or uneasy. They ignore the fear, brush it under the carpet, and pretend no one expressed it. They rush ahead. The problem is that the prospect still has fear in their system. They might go along with you to avoid conflict, but the fear will still be there at the close when you least want to see it.

You're most likely to need to use RIO Minus if the investment is more than £1,000, which I have observed to be the human fear threshold. It's for longer-term decisions. RIO Minus is my process for dealing with the prospect's concerns about:

- Risks

- Implications

- Obstacles

Risks, Implications and Obstacles mean something different for each prospect, but they have something in common: they have not happened yet and are not certain to happen.

For any decision you need to make, you could choose to focus on all the risks and all the reasons for not making it. You could have free tickets to see Andrea Bocelli, the best seats in the house, but you might be worried that you won't get a parking space near the venue or that, if you do, someone might break into your car. Those are risks, but they are not proven risks; they are not certain to happen. For some people they would be reasons to stay at home. Others would find a way around them.

An implication of this would be missing the Andrea Bocelli concert and later discovering that it was his final *ever* performance.

An obstacle is a concern the prospect has that might get in the way in the future, but, equally, it might not. None of these concerns are things that exist in the present, but the salesperson must still acknowledge them and move towards them, not away. If you ignore or dismiss any of the prospect's concerns, I promise they'll return to haunt you at close.

Get all the Risks, Implications and Obstacles out on the table and say to the prospect, 'So, you've identi-fied these possible risks that haven't happened and are not definitely going to happen; you've got some implications in your mind, which is fair enough and you're entitled to highlight them; and you can see some potential obstacles that might get in the way in the future. Now we've got a feel for all that, let's just ask ourselves: if all these things did happen, how would we get round them?'

When you've done all the problem-solving you can, you can then move on to RIO Plus. This is where you introduce the prospect to:

- Reasons to go ahead despite the issues they've identified

- Improvements that investing with you will bring

- Opportunities they will attract if they invest with you

You might say something like: 'Now, what is the one thing that would make you decide to go ahead *despite* all the potential Risks, Implications and Obstacles we've just identified? What would you need to see to make it worth going for it, even if things go wrong and the solutions we've identified don't work?'

There might still be some more fear, and you might have to go back to PUNT with a Q, back to RIO Minus, back to RIO Plus, back to PUNT with a Q. Yes, it takes time, but elite closers are prepared to commit time.

Your focus now needs to be on clearing your path to the close. The harder you work here, the easier the close will be. The more effort you save yourself now, the harder the close will be. Your ego will want to move on from this path-clearing stage, lock the call down, and then hope that they say yes. Don't listen to the ego, pick up the broom and keep sweeping until you've cleared your path.

The bigger picture: Corporate contracts

Time takes on a different meaning when you are dealing with multiple decision-makers, a big organisation, and/or big sums of money. All the factors above come into play, but they usually happen multiple times and the process takes much longer.

As I mentioned in Chapter 5, one commercial property deal took me and my brother (my business partner at that point) seven years to go from cold to sold. Three of those years were spent before the written proposal, in multiple discussions with multiple decision-makers in multiple departments, collating all the information that we could before presenting. Then it took us four years to close.

The danger is that you could be giving up all that time for free, so we had to get a commitment in the first place: a contract to say that the negotiations were going to be in good faith. But we were committed to spending that time gathering information.

When you are dealing with a complex organisation, there are a few golden rules.

Understand the multiple MAN

Identify early on who will make the final decision, what the company's process is and the culture of making decisions. You will probably not get through to the top decision-maker to start with (although this is very possible and can be done), and you will have to ask a lot of questions to understand the chain of decision-making and the culture of buying. You will need to infiltrate the system.

What do you need to know now so that you can prepare yourself and make sure you set up all the right meetings in the right places? The earlier you can find these answers, the sooner you will be working in the prospect's system rather than against it, which will release you from constantly being frustrated and let down.

As I have often said, start with the end in mind. Ask your first contact in the organisation: 'Look, just imagine that you and I were about to do business and exchange contracts, and this contract was going to get you everything you needed, and it was a great contract for me. Imagine we are exchanging. What's the process that you would normally go through to get to that point?'

They then explain the process, and you ask them about the culture: 'Well', they say, 'we have to get all seven heads of departments to sign this off'. And you go back to process: 'The last time all seven heads signed something off, what was the process to get to that point?' Then back to culture: 'What's important to each head? What are the buying teams around each head, and who's involved, and what's their culture?'

Other questions about the process might include: How does it work? How do you make decisions collectively? How many meetings would normally be involved? Who's at the meetings?

Questions about the culture might be: other than money, what would be the top five reasons that you'd go ahead? What are you looking for in a supplier like us, other than the best price?

You will probably need to do PUNT with a Q multiple times with multiple people, then RIO Minus and RIO Plus with some, then back to PUNT with a Q.

Again, this takes a lot of time, but closers move slowly. They're in control of the conversations that need to happen or don't need to happen, and they're prepared to invest the time that a long complex negotiation requires.

Agenda closing

Your aim is agenda closing or schedule closing, which is getting your ideal outcome – the close – on the agenda long before you get within reach of closing. Lock down the meetings you need in order to close ahead of getting through to the top end and presenting to the MAN so that you are always working within the prospect's system and moving towards signing. Wherever possible, you're looking to close one meeting with multiple decision-makers at the same time.

Take control of scheduling the meetings, which relieves the prospect company of a lot of hassle. You can automate a lot of this.

Once we sign a contract, I send one email, the client plugs in some information, and then the rest is automatic. All the people who need to have an exploratory call with me will show up to a group Zoom. I worked with someone who, once somebody decides to negotiate with him, sends an automated set of emails that schedule meetings with the critical team members he identified in his original exploratory conversations.

The BWP check in

Now it is time to decide whether you and the prospect are going to ride into the sunset together, or at least over the red line. If you've gathered enough, and shared enough with the prospect, deciding whether you are a match should be easy.

Here's what you need to do:

- Recap what you've told the prospect. Recap all the information that you've gathered during the prospecting journey. Repeat what they've said in their words as much as you can. This is the perfect opportunity to clarify your understanding of what you think they have said, and to confirm if they wish to amend, update or change any information shared.

- Explain in person why the product or service is right for them. Give any information they still need in person.

You can also decide at this stage:

- You are not a good match for now, but definitely could be in the future. Add them to your community, send them some helpful info for free, and ask for a referral. Leave them with a good memory.

- You aren't going to be able to help them, so you can get them out of your pipeline and recommend them to someone else. This is pipeline discipline, but you can still end on a friendly and helpful note.

Always follow the sixty-second rule (text the prospect what has been agreed or acted on within sixty seconds of the call).

It's good to talk

Never use email to negotiate or sell (in the sense of giving detailed information). Emails are written and writing cannot convey the nuance and energy that you want to express, nor are you able to respond to theirs.

I feel so strongly about this that I will not do business with people who only communicate by email. If someone is going to invest thousands of pounds with me, at some point we will need to have a powerful conversation. I will promise them an email summary of every conversation if that's what they want. If the only time they can take a phone call is 6am, I will call them at 6am. I will make it as easy as I can for them to do business with me, but I will only email them to confirm what has been agreed over the phone.

Lock down: The written proposal

Lock down is the point where, having completed all the steps above, you prepare the prospect, in a call, to expect your written proposal. You only make this call when you have done all your preparatory SQUID work, gathered all your information, and employed PUNT with a Q and RIO to ensure that you have a high chance of your proposal being accepted.

I always ask two questions at this point before sending the proposal:

1. 'Other than what we've already talked about, what other information do you need so that, when we do speak next, we can effortlessly exchange contracts?'

2. 'Who else between now and then will be involved with this decision, and what would they need to see other than what's in the written proposal so that, the next time we speak, we can effortlessly exchange contracts?'

If you're dealing with corporate contracts, you will have been aware of the multiple decision-makers and processes long before now, but even if you are dealing with a solo entrepreneur, you still need to check that there isn't a secret MAN lurking under the table.

I like to send the written proposal while the prospect is still on the lock down call after I've asked the questions. I check that they've got it, set out the options, and I do something that we'll meet again in the next chapter, on the other side of the red line, called a test close. I ask: 'Just imagine that we were about to sign now; which option do you think you'd go with?' Sometimes people say right away, 'I'm in'. If they're spending under £1,000, that can happen quite a lot. It's worth a try.

The written proposal itself should be simple, giving a few clear options. The human brain is so lazy and so full of the desire to be safe, that if you make a written proposal too wordy, too full of figures and information, too many choices, you will lose the prospect. If you are still explaining things in the written proposal ('If you put a grand here and there, and £236 there and save yourself £16, then £10 over there'), it's almost impossible for the prospect to simply say, 'I'm in'.

Don't send a bespoke email as long as your arm: state what the product or service is, the result it will deliver and the financial options. Include the Logical Next Step – what will happen when the proposal is accepted, or the contract is signed, and lock down the time for a conversation about it. Suggest a couple of dates to sign off the paperwork. Get a date in the diary.

Don't use the written proposal to solve the prospect's specific problems. That will happen once they have bought your product or service and you have fully investigated what they need. If you go to see a doctor, they don't tell you that you need heart surgery before checking your symptoms. You only have a pre-op when you've agreed what operation you're having.

Once your written proposal is submitted, you have crossed the red line. If this was *The Wizard of Oz*, you would be treading the Yellow Brick Road in Technicolor. Everything changes from here. If you have followed my process, you can stop selling and start closing. See you on the other side.

PART FOUR
AFTER THE WRITTEN PROPOSAL

In Part 1 of this book, Nick James demonstrated his expertise at the front end of growing a business: marketing, creating opportunities, personal branding, positioning. Nick has created an automated cold-to-sold system for his main business, which is selling tickets for live events. He has become an expert in closing sales online, often without any human-to-human interaction.

When Nick and I work together, my contribution is to help his team close even more sales by adding the all-important human connection to their successful online-marketing-led process.

It may be that your business is similar – that many of your clients are willing to commit to buying online – but you still need to close more sales more consistently.

It may be that prospects have shown enthusiasm for your product or service online, but they haven't taken their Logical Next Step – your training package or event ticket is still sitting in their basket.

We have established that there is a limit to what people will freely buy online. The limit will vary according to the field you are in (I have said before that, in my world, anything over £1,000 causes hindering thoughts to appear). It could be that your client has reached their discomfort zone and their discomfort cannot be solved by an automated system.

Or perhaps you have already had plenty of contact points, you have successfully coaxed and nurtured the prospect along the pipeline, locked them down and sent your written proposal, and now everything has gone quiet.

Again, it's time for some human-to-human connection. Let's do it.

8

Warm Prospect

In an ideal world you would not need this chapter. You would go straight from the Prospect stage of the journey over the red line – sending the written proposal – to the Hot Qualified Lead stage where prospects are as eager to close as you are. But life, as ever, is far from ideal, so this chapter is going to give you some tools that will be useful in the following situations:

- The prospect is firmly in your pipeline, you have even successfully delivered your written proposal and taken your prospect over the red line, but it's all gone quiet. Perhaps your prospect has missed or cancelled the call you booked in at lock down. If you didn't book a call, go back to the lock down section at the end of Chapter 7 and book a call now.

- You have excellent online marketing and your prospect is ready to buy but has not done so yet and has had no contact other than through your website.

- Your progress on the prospecting journey so far has been extra speedy (in my business, this happens a lot under £1,000). It feels as if you're ready to close but you haven't yet made your written proposal and you want to make sure the speed does not cause pre-close panic in your prospect and that they are a perfect fit.

The answer to all these predicaments is more human-to-human contact. This chapter is all about having a well-thought-through follow-up process that will give the prospect every chance to buy the product or service they need.

As well as the new tools in this chapter, which are designed to help you fire up the prospect's imagination, you can still make good use of the techniques introduced in Chapter 7 – in fact, you will need to be prepared to hop back and forth between this chapter and the previous, as there might be points where you will have to reach back over the red line to find out more information.

First, let's look at each potentially discouraging situation in turn.

'It's gone quiet': It's not them, it's you

When people come to me for advanced sales training, the number one problem getting in the way of closing more sales is their failure to follow up the prospects already in their pipeline. My number one solution is to encourage them to follow up with people who they don't know for sure aren't interested. A lull after the written proposal is common, but it does not mean your prospect has gone quiet on you. On the contrary, you have gone quiet on them.

Many salespeople do one of two disastrous things at this point. They pursue people who they haven't even qualified properly in the first place, who never really showed much interest, and become pushy and annoying, therefore ensuring they will fail. Alternatively, they give up and bow out, making an assumption along the lines of, 'Well, if they haven't got back to me by now / if they haven't bought it by now, they're obviously not interested'. That buy-or-die mentality is unhelpful, unprofessional and outdated. Here's a great question that you could add into good daily practices: 'Who do we already know that was a good match the last time we spoke, who could I approach again today?'

Decision-makers have got lots of decisions to make at any one time and it's up to you to get back to them, follow up and be purposeful, professional and persistent (as long as at some point in the past they put their hand up and registered their interested in your product or service). This purchase may or may not be a really important decision for them, but it may also be one decision in fifty they've got to make and it is now sitting on their to-do list. If you have qualified the prospect properly at the start (see Chapter 5) and they are in your pipeline, then they are interested. It's up to you to get back to them to heighten their interest.

That human-to-human interaction – getting back to people who have shown interest – is part of your job as a professional salesperson (in fact, it's your duty). It might take a lot of repeated effort and extra contact points, and you will need to be persistent, but as long as you are serving the prospect with each follow up, they won't have you arrested for it.

I recently closed a sale for £21,000 plus VAT for two people joining the top level of my training, the platinum group. I followed them up twenty-three times between sending them my written proposal (the point at which I knew they wanted to buy) and the moment their money hit my bank account (not the time they said yes – they had said yes weeks before, but it wasn't real until they'd paid).

I used a mixture of email, Facebook Messenger, Facebook voice notes, WhatsApp voice notes, WhatsApp chats and WhatsApp video. I even sent a selfie at one point because it had all gone a bit quiet, this time because of me. I was saying: 'Remember me? I'm still here. There's a reason you came towards me.'

I had to follow up twenty-three times because the client was a sales director and there were a lot of other people involved, and he had to get his team on side and get it organised. He accepted me following him up twenty-three times. He was qualified, and he wanted what I was offering, but he was so busy that I had to do the following up, I had to be in his ear. Because he's a sales director, he understood.

His last message to me before we closed was, 'I can't wait to see the back of you – but I love you (while laughing out loud)'. It really is like going on a date – you earn the right to that sort of relationship.

You might not need nearly as many contact points as that. If you locked down your follow-up process just before sending your written proposal, or at the same time, your first contact point after the red line will already be scheduled. You'll have agreed the follow up before it needed to happen.

Online only

You've got people who have moved through your pipeline online but haven't bought and haven't spoken to anyone yet.

Your system needs to include a point at which you can follow up prospects in person to supply any information they still need and to answer any genuine concerns and fears they may have.

Make that contact now and get them to take the step from engaging online to engaging in real life.

Not ready yet

You could be talking to a prospect who is interested and heading for Hot Qualified Lead status at great speed, but they've only just found out your fees. Although they seem keen to close, your approach therefore has to be softer than you would take with a Hot Qualified Lead.

There have been times when I have deliberately slowed down the speed of closing because I've seen what can happen when salespeople are impatient.

Someone comes towards your product or service and says they're interested. That's when most salespeople start talking and explaining, they don't do any listening. They don't ask any questions. The prospect hears a deluge of information, and fear comes up. They've had no time to state what they need, they're feeling pressured to close, and they're thinking, 'This salesperson is just after my money'. Then you get the excuses. We teach excuses in this context as 'neurological lying stalls'. Things like 'Do you know what? I need to have a think about it', and, 'I just can't talk at the moment, it's not a good time', or 'It's more than I want to spend'. The list is endless and well-rehearsed and said with conviction, which normally causes the salesperson to go away.

By not having professional sales skills and presuming that, just because someone says they are interested, they're just going to get their card out and pay you, you have put fear into someone who initially moved towards you. It's unbelievable how many salespeople do that.

Instead, I'm willing to take a step back, go back over the red line and use the PUNT with a Q and RIO Minus/Plus techniques to make sure my solution is right for the person. If you rush this stage, it will come back to bite you. Follow the process!

See my Warm Prospect Checklist to see how I condense the entire sales journey into one conversation plus overnight reflection

The Warm Prospect checklist

The pitfalls above won't put you off your stride if you follow my process. This is my Warm Prospect checklist which shows the steps to follow to condense the entire sales journey into one conversation, to turn a

Warm Prospect into a Hot Qualified Lead. Some will be familiar from previous chapters and others are introduced here.

Step 1: MAN

Have you checked that you are still dealing with the decision-maker? You should fully understand the decision-making process before sending a written proposal, but you need to check in here to make sure nothing has changed. Who ultimately makes the final decision?

Step 2: Logical Next Step

What is the next piece of information the prospect needs from you to become a Hot Qualified Lead? What will happen next? When will the next contact point be? If it's not going to be the lock down conversation, below (in which you prepare to close), what needs to happen before then?

Step 3: PUNT with a Q
(if the lead has been online)

You may feel that you have addressed all the points in PUNT with a Q (as a reminder – Pain, Urgency, Need and Trust, plus Qualitative Questions to draw out more precise data), but it never hurts to run through these with the prospect again if they feel that everything is moving too fast. It may be that you've missed something, or that the prospect simply needs reminding.

Step 4: Test close

This is the point where you have shared all the information that the prospect has asked for but they haven't indicated that they are not ready to close. You therefore behave as if they are ready to close, with questions such as, 'How soon do you want to get started?', 'How many tickets would you like to our event?', 'Which of our workshop dates would suit you?' These questions assume you are dealing with someone who wants to go forward with you.

The test will reveal how near they are to closing. Either they will move towards closing, or the test close will reveal some lingering fear or hindering thoughts. The test close is often when the prospect reaches for a selection of stalls to buy themselves more time: 'I'm busy right now', 'Can you email me all the details again?', 'I just need to check with someone else'.

If you don't hear any of this, and they don't outline any serious objections, you can start closing. If you do need to deal with stalls and objections, there are some scripts that will help you in Appendix 2, but we also have the next secret weapon, the flip back. This is perfect for this part of the process – it involves flipping the prospect back to the point at which they made the biggest steps towards you. There is also the flick forward approach, which we'll use in the Imagine stage, below.

Flip Back and flip forward

This is part of my powerful 'bullseye' language formula. It is designed to help you have effortless and productive sales conversations in which you listen to the prospect and find out their true needs and then use the prospect's own words so you aren't floundering around searching for the right thing to say. There are three core bullseye techniques:

- **Bullseye mirror**, in which you listen carefully to the prospect and reflect the last critical phrase that they used in your reply. For example, they might say, 'We need to save money', to which you can reply, 'How much money might you save if you...?' If they say, 'I would love to go ahead but I need to speak to my partner', you might reply, 'When you say you would love to go ahead, what is it that attracts you?'

- **Bullseye flip back**, in which you pick up on a word or phrase that the prospect uses about a point in the past when they were drawn towards your offer and add the words 'flip back' to steer them back to their positive feelings about your product. For example, they might say, 'We thought your sales training would be really great for us, but we've got a lot going on at the moment and a whole new team to set up, so...' to which you might reply, 'Just flip back with me: What was it about our training that you first thought would be great for you?'

- **Bullseye flick forward**, in which you invite the prospect to define what they would need to feel confident about in the future in order to invest with you there and then. They might say, 'We can see the results this would bring, and they look great, but it's not the right time for us now; we need to have a think about it.' In this case you might reply, 'Just flick forward with me: What results would you need to see in the next three months to make you seriously consider doing it now?'

Step 5: Lock down

As in the previous chapter, and as in every stage after the written proposal, your next contact point needs to be booked and in the diary, and a clear purpose for the call should be established, which will be in the title of the confirmation email you'll send after you've finished this conversation and been through the Warm Prospect checklist.

This is a good time to repeat the two crucial lock down questions from Chapter 7:

1. 'What other information do you need so that, when we do speak next, we can effortlessly exchange contracts?'

2. 'Who else in between now and then will be involved with this decision, and what would they need so that, next time we speak, we can effortlessly exchange contracts?'

Step 6: Imagine

This is where I use the bullseye flick forward technique. As explained above, I'll take one word, phrase or statement that the prospect uses and use it back on them. They might say, for example, 'Look, I'm probably going to go with you. I just need to check XYZ.'

In response, I'll say, 'Brilliant. Now I know you're probably going to go with me, flick forward with me. What result would you need to get so you'd definitely go with me and get rid of probably?' This is what I call 'possibility thinking', which requires a shift in mindset.

Sales		Closing	
Cold	Prospect	Warm Prospect	Hot Qualified Lead
Qualify	MAN	MAN	MAN
MAN	Community	LNS	PUNT Q
Cold prospecting	LNS	PUNT Q (online only)	Written proposal
PPQ	PUNT Q	Test close	(PUNT Q verbal)
Free catch	RIO	Flip back	Check in
Community	Check in	Lock down	RIO
Logical Next Step	Lock down	Imagine	Lock down

Caterpillar egg to butterfly

Mindset: Possibility thinking

Sales is so hard because prospects use something that isn't real and hasn't happened yet – the future – as a reason to push you away. Unskilled salespeople fall for this every time. Because they are rattled by the idea that a prospect will only 'probably' make a purchase, they try to convince the prospect that they are right or wrong about the future they are imagining.

For example, if a prospect says, 'I'm *probably* going to go ahead with you. I'm just not that sure I can get a return on investment', that's a standard negotiating tactic for somebody who's not quite ready to buy. The salesperson's skill here is to encourage the prospect to imagine the *possibilities* of working with you, rather than the *probability*. When a prospect says, 'I'll probably go with you', they're referring to an imagined future that hasn't happened yet (future fearful probability).

Well, if they can use negative probability then I'm allowed to use positive possibility. So I'll go into the future, even though it's not real, and invite the prospect to use their imagination about what's possible when they invest with me.

'Great. If you're probably going to go with me, let's flick forward for a moment. What would you need to get from investing with us in the future for you to say, "I'm getting rid of probably, I'm in"? How many more sales would you need to make during my twelve-month programme for this to be the greatest investment you've ever made in your business?'

Most salespeople don't react with 'possibility thinking', they try to get rid of 'probably' by convincing the prospect they're wrong: 'No, you'll definitely get your return'. Because the prospect doesn't want to argue with you, they'll just say, 'Pop it on an email', and you're out of the game.

When it pays to go back over the red line

Someone once came up to me after an event I was speaking at. They'd got my book, so they were in my pipeline, but they hadn't read it and they were like, 'Mate, that was so great. Thank you so much.'

I responded by asking a PPQ.

Me: 'Brilliant. Let me ask you a question: When it comes to selling, and in particular closing, what's going well right now?'

Prospect: 'Not a lot, to be honest. I'm doing a bit of this, I'm doing a bit of that.'

Me: 'Well, when you say a bit of this, a bit of that, what do you mean?' Note the bullseye mirror technique here.

Prospect: 'Well, I'm making some sales, but it feels like I'm pinning the tail on the donkey. I haven't really got a system. I'm quite good at selling and talking, but it just feels like it could go wrong every time. Basically, I'm winging it!'

Me: 'I'm glad to hear you are making some sales. So, out of not having a system and feeling like it could go wrong every time, which one bothers you the most?'

At this, he really opened up to me and I followed my system. I PUNTed him with a Q – I asked a pain/urgency/need question.

Prospect: 'Mate, I really need to get this sorted. It really is bugging me.'

Me: 'Well, look, the good news is I've got a three-day training programme. It's under £1,000. It solves all of those things you've mentioned. When do you want to come?'

It felt like he was nearly ready to close but I hadn't made a written proposal yet, so he couldn't buy it. If they can't see it, they can't buy it.

Prospect: 'Well, hang on a minute. What are the details?'

Me: 'I'll tell you what, rather than rattling everything off, let me just send you a text while you're next to me with a link on it.'

(I texted him what we call a one-pager – a form of written proposal – about the three-day training, including dates, times and what happens. I'm standing next to him while he's looking at it. He's just accepted my written proposal and crossed the red line, but he's only just found out about it. What are the chances of him getting his credit card out at the bar and paying me? Well, it's possible and it can happen under £1,000, but I'm not really looking to close someone for a grand right there and then.)

Prospect: 'I'd love to come but genuinely...' This is where standard stalls normally show up, such as, 'I can't make the dates', or 'It's more than I want to spend.'

Me: 'I'll tell you what, right? You sleep on it, and we'll have a call tomorrow.'

I'd locked him down for a call the next day and one of the team closed him for £750 plus VAT. By the next morning, he was a Hot Qualified Lead.

I also had somebody at the same event who had been to my three-day training programmes six months previously but who'd had good reasons for not moving on to the academy right away. 'I'm going to do this, but not now,' he'd said.

That day, he came over to my stand and said: 'I really want to do the academy'. Most salespeople would just try and close him straight away, but I took him back behind the red line. I said, 'Great, glad you want to do the academy. Flip back with me. Let me ask you a few questions.' I then asked him my PPQ and PUNTed him with a Q again to make sure that we were still a great match.

Once it was clear that we were, I said, 'Yeah, I can see why you want to do the academy. Let me send you a written proposal now. What are you doing tomorrow morning at 11? Come to the stand then – here are all the details.' So I'd locked him down for the next day, and he invested £8,400.

Here, I just followed the formula in Chapter 7 again. I went back over the red line, double-checked it was right for him again, PUNTed with a Q, RIO'd in, checked in, locked down a meeting the next day, sent him a written proposal while he was standing there, test closed and used imagination.

Me: 'What do you think you're going to do?' This was my test close.

Prospect: 'Look, I need to sleep on it. I'll speak to my wife. I think I'm probably going to go ahead.'

Me: 'Great. See you tomorrow at 11. Just before you go, other than what you've got there, what else do you need? What else would your partner need so that, when you discuss it, you can make an informed decision?'

The next day, we met at 11am and he said the magic words all elite closers want to hear: 'I'm in'. He signed up and paid in full.

It can be as fast as you like – but you must cover every point in the process.

9
Hot Qualified Lead

Y ou are now on the home straight, preparing for your closing call, meeting or final presentation, but first you have a final hurdle (or series of hurdles). This is call the six-tick exercise.

Every single time a salesperson doesn't close when they expected to, it'll be because at least one of the six key boxes outlined in this chapter isn't ticked.

Go through these six essentials in the order they are listed below. If one tick is missing when you've finished, get on the phone and resolve it before your final meeting: 'Hey, we've got a meeting on Wednesday and I've missed something – I've got to ask you a question'. Go back over the red line and fill in the blank or blanks. Otherwise, I guarantee the problem will surface when you're closing.

Your Hot Quality Lead checklist: The six ticks

1. **MAN:** You must be in front of a decision-maker at this point. It cannot be a closing call if they're not a decision-maker. Put the meeting back until you can have a decision-maker there. Check again that you understand the prospect's closing process and that you have followed it.

2. **PUNT with a Q online:** This is where you check that your online messages are clear and consistent. Everything – marketing emails, every Facebook Live, your website, your social profiles – must have your vision seed in it. Every contact point is obvious and has been attached to the result the prospect will get at the end. Position your fees, position what they get, and keep striving for more clarity and consistency. If anything is not clear enough, you need to resolve that with the prospect.

3. **Written proposal sent after verbal PUNT with a Q:** There must have been a powerful conversation (or conversations, depending on the size of the company) between people. If there has not been a verbal PUNT with a Q, you need to go back to the prospect and do it.

4. **You checked in before the red line:** Before you made your written proposal, you acted like a doctor, checking all the information that had been gathered, and you have decided that both parties are perfect for each other and should do business together.

5. **RIO Plus and Minus:** If more than £1,000 is at stake, check that you have acknowledged and investigated the prospect's fears and concerns as well as encouraged them to explore positives. That means taking the initiative to move towards resistance rather than ignoring it, and spending as much time on RIO Minus as RIO Plus. If you didn't RIO Minus them enough and they say, 'Well, actually, I'm still a bit worried about...', they still have some risks troubling them and you need to go back over the red line to address this.

6. **Lock down:** They are expecting the closing conversation. You've asked those crucial questions from Chapter 7 (what other information do you need? Who else will be involved and what would they need?) and you've acted on the answers. Your next meeting is to exchange contracts. Your closing meeting or call should be in the diary. It shouldn't be random, it shouldn't be out of the blue or tagged onto a call about something else. The purpose of the call – signing the contract – should be in the subject line of your confirmation email to the prospect.

If all this is in place, you should be able to close effortlessly. If one of these points is missing, go back to the relevant section under Prospect and put it in place. Remember, if even one of the ticks is missing from your list, it won't work.

Money talk

Never close on the money.

Open With a Close has a chapter on 'The 16-Digit Question', moving from close to payment. Your fee should be no surprise or problem for your prospect by this stage, so don't let the simple final hurdle of getting paid undo all your hard work.

Think ahead to what you are going to say and do at the close.

If the prospect is paying you directly by credit card, or paying a deposit to secure a booking, here are some closing questions and phrases that you can personalise according to your and their payment systems:

- 'What're the sixteen digits across your card?'

- 'How do you prefer to make the initial payment, Visa or Mastercard?'

- (If they don't have a credit card) 'Log on to your internet banking app and I'll tell you my bank details over the phone (I never text or email them) and I'll confirm when the payment's landed. Take your time, I'll wait.'

If you are sending an invoice for payment:

- 'Who's responsible for getting the invoice paid today?'

- 'Which reference or purchase order number shall I use for our invoice?'

Don't forget their Logical Next Step – how they access what they've paid for: 'Once we've got the payment confirmed, we will send you an email with all the details of X on Y date, and if you have any questions you can contact me by email/text/WhatsApp.'

Finally, don't forget to say thank you – and ask for a referral: 'Who else do you know who might be looking to dramatically increase their sales?' If they say no at this stage, don't push it and lose the sale. You can ask them at the next stage. This is about getting repeat business and collaborations from your happy customers. I call it 'milking'.

You've closed: What next?
Your milking manual

Milking is a strategy for getting more benefits from your existing clients, past or present. There is a skill to milking: cows want and need to be milked, but the amount of pressure has to be right. If you're too gentle with the cow, you won't get any milk. If you are impatient or too firm, the cow will kick your bucket over, you'll lose all the milk you had and the cow won't even let you back in the milking shed for a long time.

To milk successfully, you can use one of three strategies. You may well do at least one of these things naturally and habitually without even realising that it's a strategy, but if you make it a structured part of your process ('Who else can I call that I've worked with in the past?') and set aside time for doing it, you will get more results:

- **Sell them something else (only if it is a great fit and they would genuinely benefit from it).** Ask them if there's anything else you could possibly do for them or offer them something else that they don't even know you can do, perhaps something you've forgotten to mention: 'Did you know I also knit jumpers? Who do you know who needs a jumper in time for Christmas?'

- **Get them to refer you to someone in their network.** Ask them if they know anyone else who would benefit from any of your services.

- **Collaborate on a joint venture.** Explore the possibility of working together on something in the future.

As long as you choose just one of those three strategies at a time and follow it systematically and consistently with each individual you've worked with, you will get results and you will create a butterfly that pollinates, without having to spend anything on additional marketing or lead-creation.

Put on your 'sales skin'

By now, you should feel confident and relaxed in your 'sales skin'. It's a superhero costume rather than a dressing gown and slippers; it's familiar but it feels energising rather than cosy. As soon as you put it on, you know what to do.

Give yourself specific times during the week when you put this sales skin on: when you aren't with clients or preparing for clients, or doing marketing, or looking after operations. Ask yourself: which strategy can I employ now that's going to give me the highest return with the least effort?

Decide which one of the three milking strategies you are going to focus on for the next hour, or half hour, or less (but make it a specific length of time and set a timer). If you're going to go with 'milking: joint venture', for example, make a list of current and past clients that you have not yet spoken to about a joint venture, pick the phone up and work through the list.

If you do this, your past and present clients will also get something extra from your relationship, and together you will create opportunities that didn't previously exist, so it's a win for you both, and a win for the universe.

Conclusion

F ollowing our processes in tandem (both Nick's and Matt's), and making them your own, will bring you consistency and predictable growth for your business.

When a business's results are inconsistent, up and down, that's because it doesn't have a process. When you create consistency, you enable the business to grow and scale because you are working with numbers and data that are factual rather than hopeful.

Parts 2, 3 and 4 of this book explained how to create consistency in sales, following the overview in Part 1 about how to predictably and consistently grow and scale your business.

Just imagine that you have complete clarity, confidence and control over the numbers in your business. Imagine what that would mean for your business, removing uncertainty and freeing you up to be creative.

Because this formula is applied to the Elite Closing Academy and to Nick's mastermind programme, we can ask the head of sales every month for accurate forecasts on any of the businesses' multiple products and services. We can ask, for example, 'How many Hot Qualified Leads have we got this month for the Elite Closing Academy three-day training?'

If the answer's 30, we know there is a 90% conversion rate, so twenty-seven are likely to sign up for the three-day training shortly and three will go back to Prospect or drop out of the pipeline. We know that a certain percentage will go on to invest in the entire academy, and that a certain percentage of those who join the mastermind programme will stay for the entire experience.

Just imagine what would be possible for you and your company if you could work with numbers as specific as that.

This book has given you an outline of the professional sales skills you need to acquire to get there, but sharpening those skills needs constant reinforcement and practise. You need to commit to taking your professional practice to a higher level and investing time in it every day in order to make every sales conversation have an impact on the bigger picture.

The Elite Closing Academy's programmes take you through the process in depth, giving you constant feedback and support, building your skills until you reach the twelve-month programme, which is where you learn to make the sales magic happen.

If you'd like to find out about how we can help you make even more sales, visit:
www.eliteclosingacademy.com

You are also welcome to join Matt Elwell's free Facebook community at facebook.com/EliteClosingAcademy.

If you'd like to find out about growing your business to seven figures and beyond, visit:
www.expertempires.com

Appendix 1: Cold Calling

Matt's art of cold calling

The way I teach a cold call is, like a lot of things I have explained in this book, the opposite of the way most people do it. There are two phases to my cold calling strategy, and a five-step process to making a successful first cold call with the MAN. You can find my cold call script in Appendix 2.

You might not need to do a cold call right away. Your MAN is likely to be on LinkedIn, or perhaps for your business they're more likely to be on Facebook or Instagram, or in a professional online forum you belong to. Whatever the best route is for you, make it part of your process. Use every channel at your disposal to create a link between the MAN and your product or service. You could send them a book, a LinkedIn friend request or a voice note. Use whatever tools you have. This is my approach to cold calling on social media.

Phase 1: Find your MAN

Cold calling doesn't work for every company, but it does work for many of them. When I worked in retail, I gave myself a schedule: 'Between 1pm and 1.15pm today, I'm going to make five Phase 1 cold calls'. Phase 1 calls are simply establishing the right person to speak to.

Ring five places and have a conversation along these lines:

> **Salesperson:** 'I need some help please, I'm just on your website. Who in your organisation is responsible for the training of your (sales) staff?'
>
> **Prospect:** 'John Brown.'
>
> **Salesperson:** 'Thank you, can you put me through, please?'
>
> **Prospect:** 'He doesn't take cold calls. Here is his email address.'
>
> **Salesperson:** 'Thank you, that's great. Just before I go, who else assists him that I could possibly speak to, please?'
>
> **Prospect:** 'No one, it would be John.'
>
> **Salesperson:** 'Thank you. Bye.'

Phone down. Make five calls like that and get five names.

I taught myself to do this when I was seventeen and in my first job, selling ladies' sanitary products to businesses. I wandered into businesses at random asking if they would like to buy any ladies' sanitary products and had the results you might expect. I worked out that I needed to ask, 'Who is responsible for looking after the wellbeing of your female employees?' Then everything changed.

Phase 2: Talk to the MAN

Next, between 1.45pm and 2pm, I would make five Phase 2 calls using the names I'd gathered that morning:

'Hi, it's Dave, can I speak to James, please?'

And then, once you've been put through:

'James, you don't know me. I'm currently on your website. We are – right here, right now – the largest training company in Birmingham, that doubles the size of large coaching businesses when it comes to closing more sales.
'You can start your journey for just a few hundred quid.

'Let me ask you a question. When it comes to selling, and in particular closing, if there was one thing I could send you for free, what would that be?'

Over. It's finished. Whatever happens next is perfect, so you become detached from the outcome. I've only got one goal – to send him a book if he's interested, and if he's not, I'm cool.

Whenever you pick the phone up for Phase 1 or 2 calls you have to be ready for a call or a Zoom with the MAN. You need to grab their attention quickly, using my five steps:

1. Never sound salesy (and state your intention).

2. Make a big (true) statement worth dying for.

3. Position your fee from the start.

4. Use a Cold PPQ.

5. Lock down a Logical Next Step (or not).

Never sound salesy (and state your intention)

When you get your MAN on the phone for the first time, you've got to state your intention right away, because they don't know you. If you start talking at them straight away, you'll lose them. You must have a transparent intention.

If I get through to the MAN first time, cold, then I'll explain that I'm on their website and I'll state what I'm doing, which takes the fear away. Or, if Herbert in reception has told me that Kim is responsible for closing more sales, then I'll state my intention right out of the block: 'Kim, hello. My name is Matt. You don't know me. I've just spoken to Herbert who assures me you're responsible for training staff to close more sales.' I state my intention and let Kim know that I've got a reason for calling.

Don't say: 'It's just a quick call, I'm not trying to sell you anything'. The moment you say those words, you're lying. The buyer will activate all their ancient and ingrained defence systems, and it's all over for you.

Make a big (true) statement worth dying for

You have to join the conversation in the MAN's head quickly with a huge statement that grabs their attention. I might call a life coach and say, 'Look, I'm on your website right now and I've got an offer you might be interested in.' That's number one, intention. Now for number two, statement: 'I'm the leading sales training company in the country that doubles sales for life-coaching businesses over twelve months'.

Of course, you need to adapt the huge statement to the sector you're in or the person you're talking to, and you only say something that's true. My business does indeed regularly double (or much more than double) sales for coaches and experts. (Remember, if you can under-promise with this statement, then do so, so you can over-deliver later.)

Don't say: 'We're dealing with businesses like yours'. This will prompt the response: 'Hang on, you don't know anything about my business, so that's a lie'. You don't need to lie; you just need a huge statement.

Think about wasps. You'd probably rather not, but do. You're on the patio, having a nice cold drink with your friends on a lovely late-summer afternoon. A wasp comes over and somebody traps it in a glass and then asphyxiates it, squashes it, pulls it to pieces and kills it. Then another wasp watches its friend getting asphyxiated and ripped to pieces and killed and comes over to see what's going on, and the second wasp meets the same horrible end. Then another wasp appears, and another one and another one, and you're thinking, 'If I was a wasp, I'd stay far away from us, we're murderers.'

The wasps keep coming and coming, despite the horrible wasp destruction that they are witnessing, because the reward is worth dying for. If they can get into your glass of lemonade or cider and start sucking sugar, it's heaven. That's what a huge statement should do. It should sound worth dying for. I call it a see-saw statement; the highs make up for the lows.

Your statement should be loaded with so much sugar, and such amazing benefits, that it would stop a buyer in their tracks because you've got their attention. Say things that no one else says, do things that no one else does. Remember what Nick James said about being extreme back in Part 1?

Don't do the Sales 101 stuff, the stuff you might have been told to say: 'I'm not trying to sell you anything. I appreciate you're busy. I understand it's probably more than you want to spend.' Stop saying that stuff and instead make a powerful statement with a ludicrously massive (but true) intention, and make it with certainty and conviction.

Position your fee from the start

A lot of people are scared of money talk. Don't be: read the section on Positioning Fees in Chapter 5 and do it upfront. Let people run their money patterns while you continue to ask powerful questions and add value.

Cold PPQ

We covered this under Qualification, the first cornerstone of successful sales, in Chapter 5. Remember: assume the prospect hasn't got a problem, which allows them to confide in you that in fact they do, and what that problem or need is.

Lock down a Logical Next Step (or not)

The expectations for this first call are low. The only thing you're looking to do is create a qualified prospect who takes a Logical Next Step or who leaves your pipeline. When that is your only expectation, and you're not trying to serve, sell and close on a cold call, it takes the pressure off. You'll sound relaxed and natural, and the call will go well. You are not looking to sell anything right now.

Of course, if someone says during this first call, 'Look, I'm really glad you called. I'm looking for a new X to do Y', then you'll know what to do. If you're a Great White Shark and you've been feasting on a dead whale for a month and you're full, but then, on your way to have a little swim to the bottom of the ocean you see a herring, you're going to eat that herring despite being full, because you're a shark.

Appendix 2: The Scripts

The information in this appendix is specific to the Elite Closing Academy, however it can easily be adapted to your needs using the tips and guidance in this book.

Cold call

Phase 1: Get the decision-maker's name

Who's the MAN? The person with the:

- Money

- Authority

- Need

'Hi, I'm just on your website and really need
some help.'
'How can I help you?'
'Who in your organisation is responsible for...?'

Make sure this question is loaded with huge benefits
and has an obvious answer, for example, 'Who is
responsible for training your sales team to dramatically increase sales?'

Phase 2: Call the decision-maker

'Hi, is that (first name)?'
'Yes, who's this?'
'(First name), I'm just on your website, my
name's (first name) and I'm just calling
because...' – **state your intention.**
'I understand you're responsible for training
the sales team in the organisation. You don't
know me, but my training company specialises
in increasing sales for businesses like yours' –
make a huge statement.
'For as little as a few hundred pounds, you can
have the same' – **position your fees.**
'Let me ask you a question. When it comes to
sales, and in particular increasing the team's
skills, what's going really well right now?' –
ask a **context question.**
'Now, I know what's going well. If there was
one thing I could send you for free to help you
make even more sales, what would it be?'

By following these steps, you will connect, capture details and start the client journey, as long as they've shown some kind of micro commitment or a bit of interest.

Prospecting: Before the written proposal

Phase 1: The introduction

> 'Hi, is that (first name)?'
> 'Yes, speaking, who's that?'
> 'It's Matt.'
> 'Matt who?'
> 'Elite Closing Academy.'
> 'Oh yes, Matt, how are you?'

Always say thank you for something:

> 'Great, thanks (first name). First, I wanted to thank you so much for…'

1. Taking this call

2. Showing interest in our product

3. The opportunity to talk today

State that the purpose of your call is to ask the prospect a question. Ask an obvious question that is linked to the outcome you are trying to achieve, for example: 'Second, I have a strong reason for making this call. What made you click on the link about our…?' or

'Which one of our products or services do you believe would get you even better results or solve a problem?'

When you get an answer, the introduction phase is over and you can transition into Phase 2.

Phase 2: Prospecting PUNT with a Q Pain

- 'When it comes to (XYZ) what's your biggest challenge right now?'

- 'What else?'

- 'Out of the two answers you just gave, which one bothers you the most?'

Now you know their biggest challenge, establish the **urgency** of their problem:

- 'How long have you had this problem?' (Quantify this wherever possible.)

- 'What's going to happen if you don't solve it?'

- 'How long can you continue with this being a problem?'

- 'Who else suffers if you don't solve it?'

Now you know the biggest challenge they face and how urgent it is to solve, ask them more about their **need**:

- 'What do you think you need from us to get this sorted out quickly?'

- 'What else?'

- 'Who else needs to be involved?'

Now ascertain their **trust**:

- 'What have you seen or heard about our product or service that compelled you to come towards us?'

- 'How did you find us?'

- 'What do you know about how we can solve this?'

Qualitative questions:

Whenever your prospect answers, it's important to nail down quantifiable or measurable information. For example, if the biggest challenge they identify is needing more leads, you might ask:

- 'How many leads do you get now?'

- 'What's the conversion from those leads?'

- 'How many leads do you believe you should be getting?'

- 'How much are they worth/how much are you leaving on the table?'

Once you have collated all the data, it's time to check in and recap on the information given so far and use RIO Minus:

- 'What are the other possible risks we would need to consider before making a written proposal?'
- 'What are the possible implications of us working together?'
- 'What are the possible obstacles that we need to consider now so that we don't have them come up and halt our progress later in the deal?'

Check in on the MAN as well: 'Other than you, who else might be involved with the final decision?'

Now it's time to decide the next step:

1. It's so urgent that you need to give them details of the product that solves their urgent need and close them straight away. This will rarely be the case on a product above £1,000.

2. Make a written proposal and lock down the next action with the expectation that that is when you will close them, be it a meeting, a call or a presentation.

3. Decide they're not right for now but will be a good match in the future. Add them to your community/send them some helpful info for free/ ask for a referral.

4. Decide to unsubscribe them or recommend them to someone else who is more likely to be able to help them.

This is called 'pipeline discipline' and it's crucial for having a clean list and a pure following.

Finally:

- Always ask for a referral.

- Always follow the sixty-second rule (text them what action has been taken within sixty seconds of ending the conversation).

- Always send something that's helpful and that leaves a deep emotional memory of the interaction (a letter, a note, a video message, a written proposal, or an invite to your group on LinkedIn, Facebook, or wherever you operate).

Overcoming stalls and objections

- **'I'm busy'**: 'I understand you're busy. Let me get straight to the point. When can I come and present, Wednesday at 2 or Thursday at 3? Which one works for you?'

- **'I need to speak to my partner'**: 'Of course you do. It's critical that your partner supports the decision. Let's lock the date down and if your partner totally disagrees, we can cancel it.'

- **'I'm in but need to call you back tonight'**: 'Glad you're in, great news and thanks for confirming you will call tonight. So that I can serve you properly, let's agree a time to suit us both. How does 7.15 or 8.30 sound? Which one works best for you?'

- **'Send me an email'**: 'It's on its way, let me know when you've got it. While you're on, let me ask you a question…'

Acknowledgements

Thanks to all of our clients, customers, consumers and followers, and our amazing team here at the Elite Closing Academy HQ, for inspiring us both to share our thoughts and philosophy on how to create the perfect sales process. Thanks also to Joe Gregory and his team at Rethink Press.

Also, a huge thank you to all those who have taken the time to read this book or who are a part of my powerful community for people in business who are committed to serving others.

Matt's personal thanks go to his business partner and co-author Nick James, and to his family – his wife, Kerry, and his daughters Olivia and Eva – for always supporting him, and to Tia Smith, his personal assistant, for helping him put this book together.

The Author

Matthew Elwell is Co-founder and Director of the Elite Closing Academy and an internationally sought-after sales trainer, mentor and public speaker with clients both in the UK and globally.

Matt has thirty years' experience as an entrepreneurial business owner. His sales career has ranged from cold calling to successfully negotiating seven-figure contracts in the UK and the US. During that time, he has formulated his own philosophy when it comes to getting deals done.

In 2017, Matt turned his attention to sharing his understanding of sales and human psychology to help people sell effortlessly and with integrity, by following a process involving human-to-human communication, learned by serving over the counter in his previous family business in the retail sector.

This framework is now helping business owners to dramatically grow from start-ups to multi-six- and seven-figure businesses, and everything in between. His first book, *Open With a Close*, has been sold in nineteen different countries around the world.

In August 2018, Matt co-founded the Elite Closing Academy with Nick James which has since grown into a seven-figure business. The Elite Closing Academy was formed to give business owners, entrepreneurs and sales teams the tools required to increase their sales without coming across as pushy or manipulative. In a short space of time, the Elite Closing Academy has helped thousands of business owners all over the world to make more sales, increase their revenue and serve more people.

Matt is a family man based in Birmingham, UK. His two burning ambitions are to change the way the world sells by having the biggest sales and communication training company in the world and to continue as a self-elected ambassador for the hedgehogs of Britain.

Get started on your cold-to-sold journey now

If you want to go from being desperate for sales to having other people desperate to buy from you, we have some free resources you can get access to right now.

To ensure you're armed with the process, skills, strategies and techniques to start turning potential clients into paying customers, go to www.eliteclosingacademy.com/cold2sold